Preserves and Pickles

Preserves and Pickles

100 RECIPES FOR PRESERVING AND STORING FRUIT AND VEGETABLES

gloria nicol

RYLAND PETERS & SMALL
LONDON • NEW YORK

Project Editor: Gillian Haslam
Text Editors: Alison Bolus
and Eleanor Van Zandt
Designer: Barbara Zuñiga
Photographer: Gloria Nicol
Stylist: Sue Rowlands
Pages 93, 95, 120 and 125: photographer
Winfried Heinze; stylist Rose Hammick

First published in 2009 by Cico Books;
this revised edition published in 2021 by
Ryland Peters & Small Ltd
20–21 Jockey's Fields
London WC1R 4BW
and
341 E 116th Street
New York NY 10029

www.rylandpeters.com

ISBN: 978 1 80065 030 5

10 9 8 7 6 5 4 3 2 1

Printed in China

CIP data from the Library of Congress
has been applied for.
A CIP record for this book is available
from the British Library.

contents

why make jam?

There is something so satisfying about opening a food cupboard, pantry or larder to find the shelves stacked with colourful jars of homemade preserves. These containers of summer and autumn flavours might be just what's required to lift the mood on a dark, gloomy winter's day, when a good dollop of strawberry jam on your bread reminds you of longer, warmer, lighter days. For me, that is what making preserves is all about: capturing the essence of whatever fruit or vegetable it is and sealing that flavour in a jar for another day.

I started making jam more than 30 years ago and have always enjoyed it, despite my fair share of sticky mistakes. It is a traditional part of homemaking that celebrates the seasons and somehow makes life cosier and more comforting. My preserves are handmade and full of chunky pieces, which sets them apart from anything shop-bought. The flavours of the fruits shine through and are rarely masked with spices. Where possible, I reduce the amount of sugar, as the tarter the fruits, the fresher tasting the results.

In the current climate of concerns about being less wasteful, clocking up fewer food miles and eating seasonal, locally grown food, making preserves has never been so popular.

choosing your ingredients

Although strawberries, to give just one example, can now be bought virtually all year round, thanks to the introduction of new varieties, the use of polytunnels and the massive increase in imported produce, nothing beats the flavour of a homegrown strawberry that has ripened in the sun and been picked only moments before. It is this flavour, so sweet and intense, that can be captured in preserves.

Using your own homegrown produce for preserving is hard to beat, as the ingredients will be fresh and you will have control over their growing conditions.

Farmers' markets are another great source. You'll know that the fruit and vegetables have been grown locally and you are more likely to find unusual varieties of produce. Taking advantage of an organic box delivery scheme is another good alternative. Whatever its source, rinse all produce before use.

Food for free

Sometimes ingredients are right in front of your nose, and all you have to do is go out there and find them. Hedgerows and woodlands are full of edible fruits and berries if you know what to look for. You may find crab apples growing wild, along with damsons, greengages or blackberries. Alternatively, if you know someone who grows more fruit than they can use, offer to take it off their hands in exchange for a jar of preserve made using it. It's a win-win situation.

Fruit and pectin

For almost all fruit preserves you need to choose fresh, good-quality, just-ripe fruit in order to achieve the correct pectin content. This is because jam needs the right balance of pectin, acid and sugar to set properly. Different fruits contain varying amounts of pectin, and the pectin content is higher in just-ripe fruit. Fruits high in pectin include crab apples, red, black and white currants, Seville oranges, damsons, gooseberries

and quinces. Fruits low in pectin include strawberries, pears, elderberries, fresh apricots and cherries. Some fruits contain very little pectin, and so jams made using these fruits will need additional help to make them set. Over-ripe fruit can also lower the pectin content, which is why such fruit is not suitable for jams. It is, however, suitable for cordials, so use any fruit that is too ripe for jam to make a delicious cordial or syrup.

The pectin content can be raised in various ways: mixed-fruit jams can use the higher pectin content of one fruit to offset the lower content of another; lemon juice can be added at a rate of the juice of 1–2 lemons to every 2 kg/4 lb. 8 oz. fruit, and bottled pectin or special preserving sugar with added pectin can be used.

preserving equipment

The principle underlying all preserving is to prevent decay caused by the growth of yeasts, moulds and bacteria. These organisms are destroyed when heated to sufficiently high temperatures to sterilize them, and, once sterilized, preserves must be kept securely sealed so that air cannot enter. Preserves that contain 60 per cent or more of sugar are less susceptible to the growth of yeasts, which is why jams containing less sugar need eating more quickly.

JAM JARS

Once people discover you are a jam-maker, you will find yourself the happy recipient of empty jam jars of all shapes and sizes. Jars with screw-top lids make the best containers for jams and jellies, while jars with metal clip tops and rubber seals are perfect for potting up chutneys and pickles.

Jars need to be clean and undamaged, without any chips or cracks. Wash them in hot soapy water, then rinse in clean hot water before drying. Place the jars on their sides on a kitchen towel-covered shelf in the oven and heat to 90°C fan/110°C/225°F/Gas ¼ for 20–30 minutes, just before using them. They should come out of the oven hot and ready for filling with hot jam. Always prepare a few more jars than you think you will need (including some tiny jars to hold the last few spoonfuls from the pan) as the quantities each recipe makes may vary.

Corrosive materials must not come into contact with the preserve, especially those containing vinegar, so choose lids that will not corrode if they touch the preserve beneath. This is especially important for chutneys and pickles.

SPECIAL EQUIPMENT

There are a few items you may need for preserving:

PRESERVING PAN A non-corrosive, non-reactive preserving pan big enough to hold large quantities of boiling jam is a great investment. Also called a maslin pan, it should be wide and shallow to encourage rapid evaporation when bringing jam to setting point. A good-quality pan will have a thick, heavy base that will prevent any preserve from burning. While copper and aluminium/aluminum pans are both popular, I think stainless steel is best, and it is certainly necessary when making preserves that contain vinegar.

When jam is brought to a rolling boil it rises up in the pan, so never over-fill the pan. If the pan is too small and overfilled, you will either end up with an overflowing mess of boiling syrupy jam or, in order to prevent this happening, you won't be able to raise the temperature high enough to reach setting point.

DOUBLE BOILER Useful when making fruit curds and fruit syrups and cordials, though can be replaced by a bowl set over a pan of simmering water.

FOOD MILL A good-quality food mill with different-sized mesh discs can be used to sieve fruit to extract the purée, which is excellent for making jams and gives a pleasing texture, without 'bits'. You can also purée apples without having to peel and core them first.

JAM FUNNEL This is essential for pouring hot jam safely into jars. Choose one small enough to fit into most of your jars but wide enough not to become clogged with pieces of fruit. Sterilize and warm the funnel in the oven along with the jam jars. A sterilized, warmed scoop is useful for ladling jam into the funnel.

JAM THERMOMETER Although not essential, this is useful for testing for setting point. Choose one that goes up to at least 110°C/230°F and has a clip to attach it to the side of the pan.

JELLY BAG Ready-made jelly bags in a plastic stand that will fit over a bowl are ideal for straining the juices from cooked fruit, but you could easily make your own using muslin, cheesecloth, nylon, calico or a clean kitchen towel tied across the legs of an upturned stool (see above).

MUSLIN You will need squares of muslin/cheesecloth to hold pips, stones/pits and spices that require cooking in with jams and chutneys. A generous square of fabric can be gathered together around the ingredients and tied into a bag with natural string or twine. Alternatively, you can buy little drawstring calico bags made specifically for this purpose.

WAXED PAPER DISCS AND CELLOPHANE COVERS
Hot jam should be covered with waxed discs, placed waxed side down, immediately after bottling before the screw-top lids are put on. These help to keep the preserve sterile. The discs can be bought to fit 450-g/1-lb and 900-g/2-lb jars. Choose discs that will completely cover the jams, jellies and marmalades right to the edges where possible. The discs are often sold in packets that also contain cellophane circles, elastic bands and labels. If you have any jars without lids, these cellophane covers can be used as lids.

LABELS Label all your preserves so you know how long they have been stored. Chutneys and pickles, which benefit from a maturing period, also need to be labelled with this information.

preserving techniques

There are two basic methods for making jam. The traditional method involves cooking the fruit before adding the sugar and boiling to setting point. The macerating method requires leaving the fruit and sugar, which have a lower sugar-to-fruit ratio, together, ideally overnight, to draw out the juices and intensify the flavours, before boiling to a set. This method gives a softer-setting jam with a more syrupy consistency.

JAM: THE TRADITIONAL METHOD

COOKING THE FRUIT Place the fruit in a preserving pan with some water, the quantity of which will vary with the type of fruit. Soft fruits may not need any water, as they will quickly break up and release their juices when heated and mashed with a spoon. Harder fruits, however, will definitely need some water and a longer cooking time to soften them and release the pectin and acid. Simmer the fruits gently. Blackcurrants and plums should be cooked until their skins are soft. Once sugar is added, skins may become tough if they haven't been cooked enough before.

ADDING THE SUGAR Use white granulated sugar, or preserving sugar if the fruit needs more pectin. The amount of sugar needed varies, but the minimum amount recommended for 1 kg/2 lb. 4 oz. fruit is 700 g/3½ cups sugar. Ideally, use 750–850 g/ 3¾–4¼ cups sugar for a softer-set jam and 1 kg/ 5 cups sugar for a traditionally prepared jam.

It is best to warm the sugar in a bowl in the oven (about 20 minutes on its lowest setting) before adding it to the fruit, as this will help it to dissolve quicker. Take the jam off the heat and allow it to cool slightly so it isn't still boiling when the sugar is added. Stir continuously over a low heat until the sugar has completely dissolved. (If the jam comes to the boil before the sugar has completely dissolved, it may crystallize during storage.)

BOILING THE JAM When the sugar has dissolved, turn up the heat and bring the jam to the boil. How long it needs to boil for will vary and this is something that becomes more apparent with experience. The jam needs to maintain a high temperature to reduce and thicken so it will set as it cools. Sometimes this can take a matter of minutes and on other occasions up to half an hour, depending on how much water the jam contains. This stage is often referred to as a rolling boil.

TESTING FOR SETTING POINT After 5–10 minutes of rapid boiling, test the jam to see if it has reached setting point. This can be done in several ways (see below). Remove the pan from the heat while testing, so the jam doesn't over-cook.

The cold plate test Put a small plate in the freezer to chill beforehand. Drip a pool of jam onto the plate with a spoon and allow to cool for a few seconds, then draw your finger through the jam. If setting point has been reached, the surface will wrinkle. When you raise your finger from the plate, the jam will form a strand rather than dripping off.

Using a jam thermometer
Dip the thermometer into hot water, then push it into the jam, preferably in the centre of the pan. If the temperature reaches 105°C/220°F, setting point has been reached.

The flake test Dip a wooden spoon into the jam, then hold it above the pan. Leave it to cool for a few seconds, then let the jam fall off the spoon back into the pan. If the jam has a gloopy consistency and forms strands or flakes that hang onto the spoon, setting point has been reached.

If setting point has not been reached, place the pan back on the heat and continue to boil rapidly, testing again at 5-minute intervals.

SKIMMING During boiling, a scum sometimes forms on jam, jelly or marmalade due to bubbles rising to the surface. This scum is harmless but can spoil the appearance of the preserve. Stir in a small knob/pat of butter to help disperse the scum or use a metal spoon to scoop it away.

DISPERSING THE FRUIT Whole fruits or large pieces of fruit often rise up to the top of a jam, and, as the jam sets, they are likely to stay put. If you are making a softer-set jam with pieces in, you may have to live with this, but for a thicker set, leave the jam to settle for 5–10 minutes prior to potting up, then stir to distribute the pieces evenly.

POTTING AND STORING Have your hot jars and jam funnel ready. Pour the jam into the jars, filling them to the top. Cover them straight away with a waxed disc pushed down onto the surface of the jam and then with a screw-top lid. Leave the filled jars to cool. Jars filled to the brim can also be left to cool upside down, as this helps to produce a vacuum as it cools. Store cooled jam in a dry, cool larder or cupboard. Note that some preserves are left to go cold before being sealed – see individual recipes.

JAM: THE MACERATING METHOD

Allowing fruit and sugar to macerate together before cooking draws the moisture and juices from the fruit and preserves the flavour. Cooking times are reduced and flavours intensified, and it is possible to use a lower sugar content (see page 7), depending on the sweetness of the fruit.

Prepare the fruit as directed and place in a ceramic, glass or stainless steel bowl. Add the sugar, cover with a plate or push a piece of greaseproof/parchment paper down onto the surface of the fruit to hold in the moisture and leave to macerate: softer fruits for 6–8 hours and harder fruits for up to 36 hours. You will see the sugar soak up the juices and a considerable amount of liquid begin to dissolve the sugar.

Pour the fruit into a preserving pan and stir over a gentle heat until the sugar has completely dissolved. Occasionally, the mixture is left to macerate again, but if not, bring the jam to setting point as for the traditional method and pot up.

MAKING MARMALADE

If making citrus marmalade, it is important to cook the citrus rind properly, and this can take 1½–3 hours depending on the method you choose. Poaching the oranges whole is my preferred method, but removing the rind and shredding it at the outset is an alternative. If you use waxed fruits, you will need to scrub them before use, but just a rinse will do for unwaxed ones.

POACHING Wash the whole fruits and place in a heavy, lidded casserole with a tight-fitting lid. Pour in enough water to just cover the fruits, so they begin to float, then cover and place in an oven preheated to 160°C fan/180°C/350°F/Gas 4, to poach for 2½–3 hours, by which time the skins will be softened. Leave until cool enough to handle, then, using a spoon, lift the fruits from the liquid, halve them and scoop out the insides, gathering together all the pith and pips and collecting any juice. Slice the rind into strips. Place the pips and pith in a square of muslin and tie into a bundle with string. Pour any collected juice back in with the cooking liquid.

PARING THE RIND FIRST Cut the uncooked fruits in half, squeeze out and collect the juice. Save the pips. Pare the rind and chop into thin shreds. Chop the pith finely. Place the pips in a square of muslin/cheesecloth and tie into a bundle with string. Place everything in a pan, add enough water to cover, then leave overnight to soak. The next day, bring to the boil, then simmer for about 1½ hours until the rind is softened and cooked through. Remove the bundle of pips.

From now on, the method is the same whichever form of preparation you used. Add warmed sugar and stir to dissolve, then complete in the same way as if making jam. Once setting point is reached, leave the marmalade for 10-15 minutes, then remove the muslin bag (if using the poaching method) and stir to distribute the rind shreds before potting up.

MAKING JELLIES

A jelly is similar to a jam but does not contain pieces of fruit. The fruit is cooked with water, then poured into a jelly bag and allowed to drip through. Only the juice is made into a preserve. Fruits most suited to jelly making generally have a high pectin content (see page 7).

When making jellies, cook the fruit first with water until tender. You can mash the fruit with a spoon at this stage before pouring it into a jelly bag suspended over a container to catch the drips. For the clearest jelly, allow plenty of time for the juice to drip through (overnight is ideal), and don't squeeze the bag, as this will make the jelly cloudy. (It is often possible to re-boil the contents of the jelly bag using half the original amount of water and pour it through the bag again to get the maximum amount of juice and pectin from the fruit.)

Now measure the juice to work out how much sugar will be needed. The general rule is 450 g/2¼ cups sugar to every 600 ml/2½ cups juice, which will make roughly 750 g (1 lb. 10 oz.) jelly. Place the juice in a preserving pan and add warmed sugar as for jam-making, stirring until completely dissolved. Bring to a rapid boil and cook on a high heat to reach settting point, as before.

Rather than waste the residue in the jelly bag, push it through a food mill, collect the purée and sweeten it, to use for pie fillings or to make into another preserve.

MAKING CURDS

Fruit curds have shorter keeping times than jams and jellies: just 2 months unopened in a cool place. Make them in small jars, as once opened they should be kept in the fridge and eaten within 2 weeks. You can also pour curds into suitable containers and freeze for 6 months.

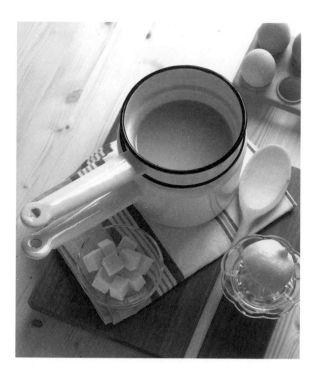

Curds are made using sugar, butter and eggs and so are more like a custard than a jam. They are best suited to tart, fruity flavours. So that the eggs don't curdle or cook on too high a heat, it is best to use a double boiler or a basin set over a pan of simmering water. You may have to stir the curd continuously for 20–30 minutes until it thickens and will coat the back of the spoon, but the result will be worth the effort.

Prepare a fruit purée first by cooking the fruit in the minimum amount of water, if any at all, until tender. Softer fruits such as raspberries and blueberries require hardly any cooking, while gooseberries and squash need more. Press the fruit through the fine disc of a food mill or a sieve and collect the purée.

MAKING CHUTNEYS AND PICKLES

Chutneys can be made from fruits and vegetables mixed with vinegar, sugar and spices. They are easy to make, generally just requiring all the ingredients to be thrown together in a preserving pan and cooked for a couple of hours. It is important to pot up in jars with vinegar-proof lids. Try to leave chutneys and pickles to mature for 6–8 weeks or even a few months before eating, as the flavours mellow over time. Pickles and chutneys both require vinegars flavoured with spices, and all the recipes in this book give instructions for making these from scratch. However, you can also make your own vinegars using the following recipes – two for pickling vinegars and two for sweetened pickling vinegars, which are suitable for pickling fruits and fruit chutneys.

PICKLING VINEGAR

To 1 litre/4¼ cups cider, malt or wine vinegar, add:
20 g/¾ oz. fresh root ginger, peeled and finely sliced
1 tablespoon each black peppercorns, mustard seeds, celery seeds
8 dried red chillies/chiles
2 teaspoons each whole allspice, whole cloves, whole coriander seeds

Mix all the spices together and divide between clean, sterlilized bottles. Top up the bottles with the vinegar and seal with corks or stoppers. Leave to infuse for 6–8 weeks, giving the bottles an occasional shake. Strain the spices from the vinegar before using.

For a quicker version:

Place all the ingredients in a bowl and place over a pan of simmering water, or use a double boiler. Allow the vinegar to warm through without boiling, then remove it from the heat and leave the spices to steep in the warm vinegar for 2–3 hours. Strain the spices from the vinegar before using.

SWEET PICKLING VINEGAR

To 1 litre/4¼ cups cider, malt or wine vinegar, add:
1 cinnamon stick
1 tablespoon each whole allspice, whole coriander seeds, whole cloves, white peppercorns
5 blades of mace
2 dried red chillies/chiles (optional)
800 g/4 cups brown or white sugar

Mix the spices together and divide between clean bottles. Warm the vinegar and dissolve the sugar in it, then top up the bottles with the vinegar and seal with corks or stoppers. Leave to infuse for 6–8 weeks, giving the bottles an occasional shake. Strain the spices from the vinegar before using.

For a quicker version:

Place 600 ml/2½ cups white wine vinegar, 200 g/ 1 cup sugar, 1-cm/⅜-inch square piece of fresh root ginger, a few whole allspice berries and black peppercorns in a pan and stir over a low heat to dissolve the sugar. Turn up the heat and boil for 1 minute, then remove from the heat. Strain the spices from the vinegar before using.

MAKING CORDIALS AND SYRUPS

Cordials, nectars and syrups make good use of fruit that is over-ripe and not suitable for jam-making; they are also easy to make. Soft fruits such as blackberries, blackcurrants, loganberries and raspberries are suitable, as are citrus fruits and foraged fruits such as rosehips, elderflowers and elderberries.

For all soft fruits the method is the same. Put the fruit in a bowl and break it up with a spoon, then add only the minimal amount of water, if any at all. Place the bowl over a pan of simmering water and heat through to extract all the juice from the fruit. Pour the fruit through a jelly bag and collect the juice underneath, leaving it to drip overnight.

Add 350 g/1¾ cups sugar to every 500 ml/2 cups plus 2 tablespoons juice and stir together over a low heat until dissolved; do not allow it to boil. Strain into clean bottles, filling to within 2.5 cm/1 inch of the top of the bottle. Cork securely or use bottles with ceramic stoppers and wires. The bottles will now need to be sterilized so that they keep for a long time. (Or, for an easier option, the syrup or cordial can be poured into suitable containers and frozen.)

To sterilize, place some folded newspaper or a trivet in the bottom of a pan and place the bottles on top. Add cold water almost to the top of the bottles, then bring to the boil and simmer for 20 minutes. Make sure that the bottles are securely sealed, then store them in a cool, dry place.

KEEPING TIMES

The jams and jellies will keep, unopened, in a cool, dark place for at least 6 months, and the other preserves will keep for 6–12 months. Keeping times will vary once jars and bottles are opened, but you'll find that these preserves are so delicious that they will be eaten up long before there is any chance of them deteriorating.

PROBLEM SOLVING

Why jam goes mouldy

Mould is most often caused by a failure to cover the jam with a waxed disc while it is still very hot. Alternatively, jars may have been damp or cold when used, weren't filled right to the top or have been stored in a damp place. Other possible causes are insufficient evaporation of water during the preliminary cooking and/or too short a period of boiling after the sugar has been added. Jam with a good set is less likely to go mouldy, while a softer-set jam will be more inclined to spoil. Sometimes mould can form because the fruit was picked on a wet day. Mould is not harmful to the jam but it may affect the taste slightly. If it is removed, the jam can be boiled up again and re-potted in clean, sterilized jars.

Why tiny bubbles appear

Bubbles indicate fermentation, which is usually the result of too little sugar in relation to the quantity of fruit. When jam is not reduced sufficiently, this can also affect the proportion of sugar.

Why fruit rises in the jam

When the fruit is in big pieces or used whole, such as strawberries, the pieces tend to rise in the jam after potting. To keep them dispersed throughout the preserve, leave the jam in the pan for 10–15 minutes after setting point is reached to thicken slightly, then stir before pouring it into the pots. The syrupy consistency of softer-set jams means that fruit will invariably rise. The same problem may occur with rind in marmalade – the solution of waiting and stirring is the same.

Why jam crystallizes

Too much sugar or too little acid are usually the cause. Low-acid fruits benefit from the addition of acid in the form of lemon juice. Making sure that the sugar has dissolved completely before bringing the jam to a fast boil also helps. Sometimes over-ripe fruit is responsible or storing the jam in too warm a place.

Why jam won't set

Low levels of pectin due to using fruits containing very little pectin or over-ripe fruit make it difficult to reach setting point. Other reasons include under-boiling the fruit, so the pectin is not fully extracted, or insufficient evaporation of the water before the sugar is added, in which case return the jam to the preserving pan and boil it further. It is also possible to over-cook jam after sugar has been added, for which there is no remedy. For fruits low in pectin, such as strawberries and cherries, you can add more pectin in the form of fruits (such as lemon juice, apples or redcurrants), bottled pectin or preserving sugar, which has added pectin.

Why jam shrinks in the jar

Shrinkage is caused by the jam being inadequately covered or sealed or failure to store it in a cool, dark and dry place.

jams

We need jam to spread on our bread, make a filling for a sponge cake and to ooze over a steamed pudding. Jam is simply a term used to describe fruit and sugar cooked together so it will keep, and can include the fruit in pieces or be made from puréed fruit. The result is one of life's sweet little extras.

Makes about 1.2 kg/3¾ cups
1 kg/2 lb. 4 oz. blackberries
1 star anise
3 cloves
1 small cinnamon stick
juice of 2 lemons
700 g/3½ cups warmed sugar (see page 10)

spiced blackberry jam

I don't often choose to spice up the fruits when jam making, preferring the simple fruit flavours to dominate. However, here a handful of warming spices suits this autumnal foraged fruit preserve down to the ground.

1 Place the blackberries in a saucepan with the star anise, cloves, cinnamon stick and 2 tablespoons water (just enough so the fruit doesn't catch on the base of the pan). Bring them to simmering point and continue cooking until they are tender and juicy, mashing them with a spoon.

2 Remove the cinnamon stick and press the berries through the fine disc of a food mill or a sieve/strainer. If you prefer a chunkier-textured jam, there is no need to purée the fruit at all: simply remove the spices with a spoon and continue with the whole blackberry pulp.

3 Add the lemon juice to the blackberries and place them in a preserving pan; heat through, stirring gently. Add the warmed sugar to the pan and stir until completely dissolved, then turn up the heat and boil the jam rapidly to reach setting point (see page 10). Skim if necessary (see page 11).

4 Pour the jam into hot, sterilized jars (see page 8) and seal (see page 11).

Makes about 1.5 kg/4¾ cups
900 g/2 lb. blackberries
1 star anise
3 cloves
1 small cinnamon stick

4 nectarines (approx. 430 g/15 oz.
   when skinned and stoned/pitted)
juice of 2 lemons
900 g/4½ cups warmed sugar (see
   page 10)

spiced blackberry & nectarine jam

I discovered this combination when I found a bargain pack of nectarines at the supermarket. They bring a welcome sharpness to the mellow flavour of blackberries as well as an appealing texture.

Cook and purée the blackberries and spices as in steps 1–2 on page 16. To skin the nectarines, place them in a bowl and pour boiling water over them. Leave for a few minutes, then drain off the water and replace with cold water; the skins should slip easily off the fruit. Cut the nectarines into quarters, removing the stones/pits, then cut each quarter into thirds (smaller pieces if you like a finer-textured preserve). Place the blackberries, lemon juice, nectarines and sugar in a preserving pan and cook as in step 3 on page 16. Leave the jam for 5 minutes, then stir to redistribute the nectarine pieces. Pot and seal the jam as before.

Makes about 1.3 kg/3¾ cups
1 kg/2 lb. 4 oz. apricots
800 g/4 cups sugar
juice of 1 lemon

apricot jam

This apricot jam contains slightly less sugar than most, resulting in a softer set, and the apricots are left in big chunks. Because of this, it is inevitable that the fruit will rise to the top of the jar, rather than being suspended evenly throughout the jam. No matter: you can simply allocate an apricot half for every serving. One apricot piece will squash perfectly under the knife to fill a scone, for example. The cooking time is kept to a minimum, so keeping the flavour at its utmost.

1 Skin the fruits by placing them in a bowl, pouring boiling water over them and leaving them for a few minutes, then replacing the hot water with cold. The skins should then be easy to peel away. Keep the skins to one side. Halve the fruits and remove the stones/pits. Place the skins and stones in a piece of muslin/cheesecloth and tie it into a bag with string.

2 Place the sugar and lemon juice in a ceramic or glass bowl and add 200 ml/¾ cup water; tuck the muslin bag in among the other ingredients. Push a piece of parchment paper down onto the surface to cover it and leave the bowl in the fridge overnight.

3 By the next day the juice will have been drawn out of the fruits into the sugar, which will be partly dissolved. Pour the contents of the bowl into a preserving pan and heat gently, stirring all the time until the sugar has completely dissolved. Simmer gently for 10 minutes without stirring so the apricot halves stay intact, then remove them from the syrup using a slotted spoon. Remove and discard the muslin bag.

4 Bring the syrup to the boil and boil rapidly to reach setting point (see page 10), then quickly put the apricots back into the syrup and bring to the boil again. Remove the jam from the heat. Skim if necessary (see page 11).

5 Spoon the apricots into hot, sterilized jars (see page 8), dividing them equally, then pour the syrup over them, filling the jars up to the top. Seal the jars (see page 11) and leave them to cool upside down.

Makes about 1.3 kg/3¾ cups
1 vanilla pod/bean
1 kg/2 lb. 4 oz. apricots

800 g/4 cups sugar
juice of 1 lemon

apricot & vanilla jam

This combination seems so French to me. With its softer syrupy set, you may be tempted to eat this delicious preserve as a dessert without the need for any bread – just add a dollop of crème fraîche.

First slice the vanilla pod/bean in half lengthways and scrape out the seeds with the blade of a knife. Then follow the instructions for Apricot Jam, adding the seeds to the ingredients when placing them in a bowl and tucking the pod pieces in among the fruit before leaving the mixture to macerate overnight. Remove the pod pieces before filling and sealing the jars.

Makes about 1.3 kg/3¾ cups

1 kg/2 lb. 4 oz. whitecurrants
4 red gooseberries (optional)
juice of 1 lemon
2 red chillies/chiles (or more if you wish),
    deseeded and finely chopped
warmed sugar (see page 10; for quantity
    see step 3)

whitecurrant & red chilli jam

Whitecurrants are another fruit with a lovely tart flavour, which makes them just perfect for jam making. This jam, with its additional chilli/chile kick, is subtle enough to eat on sourdough toast for breakfast, but could also be taken up a notch by adding more chilli to taste and serving as a relish to go with cheese. And if you have a few red gooseberries to add to the currants, they'll give this jam a beautiful rose hue.

1 Strip the whitecurrants from their stalks by running the tines of a fork through their stems. Place the currants and gooseberries, if using, in a pan along with the lemon juice and 150 ml/⅔ cup water. Simmer until the fruits are soft and bursting.

2 Push the fruit through the fine disc of a food mill or a sieve/strainer, collecting the resulting purée in a measuring jug/pitcher.

3 Allow 450 g/2¼ cups sugar to every 600 ml/2½ cups of purée.

4 Gently heat the purée and add the chopped chillies/chiles, then the warmed sugar. Stir the jam over a low heat until the sugar has completely dissolved. Turn up the heat and boil rapidly to reach setting point (see page 10). Skim if necessary (see page 11).

5 Pour the jam into hot, sterilized jars (see page 8) and seal (see page 11).

Makes about 1.3 kg/3¾ cups
1 kg/2 lb 4 oz. raspberries
juice of 1 lemon
800 g/4¼ cups warmed sugar (see page 10)

raspberry jam

Some people like jam with lots of seeds in it; some don't. With raspberry jam you have a choice. If you love the flavour of this fruit but find the seeds annoying, push the softened fruit through a sieve/strainer for a smoother finish – the result will taste just as good.

1 Place the raspberries and lemon juice in a preserving pan. Heat them gently to draw out the juice, mashing the berries with a spoon until the fruit is soft and there is plenty of juice. If you want a smooth jam, push the fruit through a sieve/strainer to remove the seeds.

2 Add the warmed sugar to the fruit and stir over a gentle heat until the sugar has completely dissolved. Turn up the heat and bring the jam to a fast boil until it reaches setting point (see page 10). Skim if necessary (see page 11).

3 Pour the jam into hot, sterilized jars (see page 8) and seal (see page 11).

Makes about 1.5 kg/5 cups
450 g/1 lb. gooseberries
450 g/1 lb. strawberries, hulled
900 g/4½ cups warmed sugar (see page 10)
juice of 1 lemon

strawberry & gooseberry jam

Gooseberries and strawberries make a good partnership as the higher pectin levels found in gooseberries offset the lower levels in the strawberries. My personal preference is also for a jam which not only tastes great but that is colourful as well, and this unusual combination certainly ticks all those boxes.

1 Place the gooseberries in a preserving pan with 3 tablespoons water. Heat gently and simmer until the berries are just soft, then add the strawberries. Cook for 5 minutes until the fruits begin to lose their shape and the juice starts to run.

2 Add the warmed sugar and the lemon juice to the fruit. Stir gently over a low heat until the sugar has completely dissolved. Turn up the heat and boil rapidly to reach setting point (see page 10). Skim if necessary (see page 11).

3 Pour the jam into hot, sterilized jars (see page 8) and seal (see page 11).

Makes about 1.3 kg/3¾ cups
1 vanilla pod/bean
1 kg/2 lb. 4 oz. strawberries, hulled;
   larger fruits halved
750 g/3¾ cups sugar
juice of 3 lemons

strawberry & vanilla jam

Let's face it, strawberry jam is the real classic. This fragile fruit isn't a great keeper, so for the best jam, capture the fruit at its freshest, preserving it in recognizable chunks. This really is summer in a jar. Here I have teamed strawberries with vanilla, the perfect partner, which as far as I'm concerned you can't ever get enough of.

   This recipe uses slightly less sugar than a traditional strawberry jam might and consequently has a softer set, which means if you are feeling really gluttonous, you can eat it straight from the jar. Or swirl a few spoonfuls through a mixture of mascarpone and plain yogurt for a fast dessert. Or dollop it onto a freshly baked scone or biscuit, eating it quickly before the jam oozes away over the sides.

1 Split the vanilla pod/bean lengthways into four pieces and place in a bowl with the strawberries, tucking the pod pieces in among the fruit. Cover with the sugar and leave for 12 hours or overnight.

2 Pour the fruit, vanilla pod and juice into a preserving pan and add the lemon juice. Cook over a low heat until the sugar has dissolved, stirring only now and then so that the fruit stays intact. Turn up the heat and boil rapidly to reach setting point (see page 10). Skim if necessary (see page 11).

3 Remove the vanilla pod pieces, scrape the seeds out of them and add these to the jam, disposing of the pods. Stir the seeds through the jam.

4 Pour the jam into hot, sterilized jars (see page 8) and seal (see page 11).

Makes about 750 g/2½ cups
450 g/1 lb. plums, halved and stoned/pitted
450 g/2¼ cups warmed sugar (see page 10)

plum jam

Where I live we have our own locally grown plum variety, the Blaisdon Red plum, so naturally that is my own particular favourite for this jam. Most years, come late summer, the trees are dripping with them, so there is always lots of jam making to be done. Of course, other plum varieties will do just as well.

1 Place the plums in a pan with 100 ml/7 tablespoons water and bring to a simmer, then cook gently for 10 minutes until the plums are soft but still intact.

2 Add the warmed sugar to the fruit and stir over a low heat until all the sugar has dissolved, then turn up the heat and boil rapidly to reach setting point (see page 10). Skim if necessary (see page 11).

3 Pour the jam into hot, sterilized jars (see page 8) and seal (see page 11).

damson jam

Damsons make superb jam, one of the best. It is an old-fashioned fruit, which isn't so often used commercially for preserving. The bold and traditional character of this fruit makes it ideal as a single fruit jam.

Follow the recipe for Plum Jam using damsons, but do not attempt to remove the stones/pits before cooking. Spoon off any stones that float to the surface, then leave the cooked fruit to cool before using your hands to find and remove the rest. Once you are sure you have removed all the stones, add the sugar and bring to setting point as above.

Makes about 1.5 kg/5 cups
450 g/1 lb. plums, halved and
stoned/pitted

450 g/1 lb. marrow/squash flesh,
cut into chunks
900 g/4½ cups sugar

plum & marrow jam

A great jam to help make just a few plums go a long way. Marrow acts as a chameleon here, bulking out the jam and soaking up the fruity sweetness of the plums.

Put the plums and marrow together in a pan with 100 ml/7 tablespoons water and continue as for Plum Jam.

Makes about 1.65 kg/5 cups
700 g/1 lb. 9 oz. raspberries
700 g/1 lb. 9 oz. ripe peaches (about 6)
1 kg/5 cups sugar
juice of 2 large lemons

peach & raspberry jam

This jam is not only wonderfully fragrant but also gloriously colourful, with a combination of deep red raspberries dotted through with peach pieces. Here, as usual, I would opt for a chunky texture to set this preserve apart from anything you will ever find in a store. You can, of course, chop the peaches finer if you prefer.

1 Place the raspberries in a pan. Warm them gently to soften them and release their juice, mashing them with the back of a spoon.

2 When they are soft and juicy, push them through the fine disc of a food mill or a sieve/strainer.

3 Place the raspberry purée, 500 g/2½ cups of the sugar and half of the lemon juice in a pan and bring to a simmer, then remove from the heat and pour into a ceramic or glass bowl. Cover the surface with parchment paper, pushed down onto the fruit, and leave the bowl in the fridge overnight.

4 Meanwhile, to skin the peaches, place them in a bowl and pour boiling water over them. Leave to steep for a few minutes, then pour off the water and replace with cold water; the skins should now easily peel away from the flesh. Cut the peaches into quarters and remove the stones/pits, then cut each quarter in half, so the pieces are still quite chunky.

5 Place the peaches, remaining sugar and lemon juice in a pan, bring just to simmering point, then remove from the heat. Pour the fruit into a glass or ceramic bowl and cover it with greaseproof paper as described for the raspberries; leave in the fridge overnight.

6 The next day, combine the raspberries and peaches in a preserving pan and heat gently, stirring all the time to be sure the sugar has completely dissolved. Turn up the heat and boil rapidly until setting point is reached (see page 10). Skim if necessary (see page 11). Leave for 5 minutes, then stir to distribute the peach pieces. Pour the jam into hot, sterilized jars (see page 8) and seal (see page 11).

Makes about 900 g/3 cups
700 g/1 lb. 9 oz. cherries
500 g/2½ cups warmed sugar (see page 10)
1 tablespoon lemon juice

cherry jam

You can use a black cooking cherry, such as a Morello cherry for this jam, or a paler dessert cherry and the colour of your jam will vary accordingly. If you grow your own, make sure to pick them as soon as they ripen or else the birds will eat the lot before you get the chance.

1 Stone/pit the cherries over a basin to catch any juice. Place the stones/pits in a piece of muslin/cheesecloth and tie it into a bag with string. Put the fruit and juice in a pan with 2 tablespoons water and simmer gently until the fruit is just cooked.

2 Add the warmed sugar and the lemon juice to the fruit and stir over a low heat until all the sugar has dissolved, then turn up the heat and boil rapidly to reach setting point (see page 10). Remove the muslin bag and leave the jam for 5–10 minutes, then stir to redistribute the cherries. Skim if necessary (see page 11).

3 Pour the jam into hot, sterilized jars (see page 8) and seal (see page 11).

Makes about 2.5 kg/8 cups
250 g/9 oz. rosehips
250 g/9 oz. hawthorn hips ('haws')
250 g/9 oz. rowan berries
250 g/9 oz. sloes

450 g/1 lb. crab apples or tart cooking
    apples, chopped
450 g/1 lb. blackberries
450 g/1 lb. elderberries
125 g/1 cup hazelnuts, shelled and
    chopped
warmed sugar (see page 10; for quantity
    see step 3)

hedgerow jam

Foraging is such a satisfying pursuit – gathering food for free that has required no effort whatsoever to cultivate. Whether there is any produce to be had is entirely in nature's hands, and the autumnal fruits may well be either bountiful or scarce, varying from year to year. Hedgerow jam makes use of lots of ingredients, but the medley can be changed based on what is readily available. As not all of the fruits for this recipe may be ripe at just the same time, you will need a flexible approach. Sloes are generally best picked after a first frost, by which time elderberries will have been and gone. Of course, not all berries are edible, so if you don't know how to recognize the ones that are, then this jam isn't for you. Hedgerow Jam is autumn in a jar.

1 Pick over the fruit and remove the stalks. Place the hips, haws, rowan berries, sloes and apples in a pan with just enough water to cover the fruit, so it just begins to float. Simmer for approximately 15 minutes until the fruit is soft and the apples fluffy.

2 Push the fruit mixture through the fine disc of a food mill or a sieve/strainer and collect the puréed pulp in a preserving pan. Add the blackberries, elderberries and nuts and simmer for 15 minutes.

3 Measure the cooked fruit and add an equal amount of warmed sugar. Stir over a low heat until all the sugar has dissolved, then turn up the heat and boil rapidly to reach setting point (see page 10). Skim if necessary (see page 11).

4 Pour the jam into hot, sterilized jars (see page 8) and seal (see page 11).

Makes about 1.3 kg/4 cups
1 kg/2 lb 4 oz. pears, peeled, cored
    and cut into chunky slices
juice of 2 lemons
750 g/3¾ cups sugar
1 vanilla pod/bean

pear & vanilla jam

This jam is another of my particular favourites and is one I find it hard to live without. The specks of real vanilla dotted throughout the pale jam show its quality, infusing their aromatic flavour. Here, macerating the pears also brings out the most flavour from the fruit.

1 Place the pears in a bowl with the lemon juice to stop them discolouring. Sprinkle the sugar over the fruit and add 200 ml/¾ cup water.

2 Slice the vanilla pod/bean in half lengthways and scrape out the seeds, then tuck the pod in among the pears and add the seeds. Cover the bowl with a plate and leave overnight for the sugar to soak up some of the juices from the fruit.

3 The next day, pour the contents of the bowl into a preserving pan and stir over a low heat until the sugar has dissolved, then turn up the heat and boil rapidly to reach setting point (see page 10), by which time the pear pieces will be translucent. Skim if necessary (see page 11).

4 Remove the vanilla pod, then pour the jam into hot, sterilized jars (see page 8) and seal (see page 11).

pear & chocolate jam

After travelling in France, my neighbours brought back some pear jam which had tiny nuggets of chocolate suspended through the syrup. This is my interpretation of that unusual preserve.

Coarsely grate 150 g/5 oz. good-quality dark/bittersweet chocolate. Make the Pear & Vanilla Jam and spoon it into the jars in layers interspersed with sprinkled grated chocolate. The chocolate will melt on contact with the hot jam, but the aim is to have chocolate speckled throughout, rather then mixed in, so that the overall colour of the jam is pale.

Makes about 1.65 kg/6 cups
1 kg/2 lb. 4 oz. pumpkin or butternut
  squash flesh
1 vanilla pod/bean
1 kg/5 cups sugar
juice of 2 lemons

pumpkin & vanilla jam

This recipe is a great one to make when you are faced with a pile of scooped-out pumpkin innards after making Halloween lanterns. The natural sweetness of the pumpkin flesh is just perfect for making into jam.

1 Place the pumpkin flesh in a pan with just enough water to stop it catching and cook over a moderate heat for 10–15 minutes until it is cooked through but still retains its shape. Drain off any excess juices and, when the pumpkin is cool enough to handle, chop it into finer pieces.

2 Slice the vanilla pod/bean in half lengthways and scrape out the seeds with the blade of a knife. Place the pumpkin, sugar and lemon juice in a bowl, tuck the vanilla pod pieces in among the pumpkin and add the seeds. Cover with a piece of parchment paper pushed down onto the surface and leave overnight.

3 The next day, pour the contents of the bowl into a preserving pan and stir over a low heat until all the sugar has dissolved, then turn up the heat and boil rapidly to reach setting point (see page 10). Skim if necessary (see page 11).

4 Pour the jam into hot, sterilized jars (see page 8) and seal (see page 11).

Makes about 1.3 kg/4 cups
500 g/1 lb. 2 oz. apricots
500 g/1 lb. 2 oz. rhubarb, cut into short lengths
750 g/3¾ cups sugar
juice of 1 lemon

rhubarb & apricot jam

This jam is an absolute star. Everyone who has tasted it has been knocked out by how full of flavour it is and the perfection of this combination of fruits. The pinkness of the rhubarb pieces along with the chunky apricot halves also makes it a real treat visually. If you make only one jam in this book (hopefully you'll make more than that!), this is the one.

1 Skin the apricots by placing them in a bowl and pouring boiling water over them. Leave for a few minutes, then drain the water and replace with cold water. The skins should then be easy to peel away with a knife. Cut into halves and remove the stones/pits.

2 Place all the ingredients in a bowl, cover with a plate and leave for 1 hour.

3 Pour the contents of the bowl into a preserving pan and stir over a low heat to dissolve the sugar. Turn up the heat and bring just to simmering point, then remove from the heat. Pour everything into a glass or ceramic bowl, cover with a piece of parchment paper pushed down onto the surface and leave overnight in the fridge.

4 The next day, pour the contents of the bowl back into the preserving pan and stir over a low heat until all the sugar has dissolved, then turn up the heat and boil rapidly to reach setting point (see page 10). Skim if necessary (see page 11).

5 Pour the jam into hot, sterilized jars (see page 8) and seal (see page 11).

Makes about 1.4 kg/4½ cups
1 kg/2 lb. 4 oz. rhubarb, cut into short lengths

finely grated zest and juice of 3 limes
850 g/4¼ cups sugar

rhubarb & lime jam

Rhubarb is often teamed up with orange, but I much prefer to combine it with lime instead. This is a medley made in heaven.

Place all the ingredients in a bowl, cover with a plate and leave for 1 hour. Then follow steps 3–5 of Rhubarb & Apricot Jam.

Makes about 750 g/2½ cups
450 g/1 lb. figs, stalks removed and
chopped into small pieces

450 g/2¼ cups warmed sugar (see
page 10)
juice of 1 lemon

green fig jam

Green or purple figs are suitable for jam making. Figs do not ripen any further once picked from the tree, and they don't have a massive flavour when unripe, so pick or buy them already ripe enough to use. This jam has a beautiful rich colour and is dotted throughout with seeds.

1 Place the figs in a pan with 2 tablespoons water, heat gently to a simmer and cook until soft and juicy.

2 Add the warmed sugar and the lemon juice to the fruit and stir over a low heat until all the sugar has dissolved, then turn up the heat and boil rapidly to reach setting point (see page 10). Leave for 10 minutes, then stir to distribute the fig pieces throughout the jam. Skim if necessary (see page 11).

3 Pour the jam into hot, sterilized jars (see page 8) and seal (see page 11).

Makes about 1.4 kg/4½ cups
600 g/1 lb. 5 oz. figs
400 g/14 oz. pears, peeled, cored
and diced

finely grated zest and juice of
1 large orange and 1 lemon
850 g/4¼ cups sugar
8 green cardamom pods, crushed
and pods discarded

fig & pear jam

Both main ingredients here are low in pectin so definitely need help from the lemon and orange additions to boost their setting power. Green cardamom seeds add a unique and unusual twist.

Prepare the figs as above, then place all ingredients in a bowl and leave for 1 hour. Pour into a preserving pan, stir over a low heat to dissolve the sugar. then turn up the heat and bring to simmering point. Pour into a glass or ceramic bowl, cover with parchment paper pushed down onto the surface and leave overnight in the fridge. Next day, pour the contents back into the pan and stir over a low heat, then turn up the heat and boil rapidly to reach setting point (see page 10). Pot as above.

Makes about 700 g/2 cups
finely pared rind and juice of 1 lemon
500 g/1 lb. 2 oz. green tomatoes, finely
    chopped
400 g/2 cups sugar
2 pieces of stem ginger, finely sliced

green tomato jam

Usually thought of as an ingredient for chutney, green tomatoes were once popular for jam making but have somehow fallen from favour. This recipe will prove that a fashion revival is due. The lemon rind and stem ginger work well here to produce a candied jam with a fabulous colour.

1 Place the rind in a pan with just enough water to cover it and simmer for about 1 hour until soft. Drain the rind, discarding the liquid.

2 Place the tomatoes and lemon juice in a bowl with the sugar and leave overnight for the sugar to soak up some of the juices from the fruit.

3 Next day, pour the contents of the bowl into a preserving pan and add the rind. Stir over a low heat until the sugar has dissolved, then turn up the heat and boil rapidly to reach setting point (see page 10). Skim if necessary (see page 11).

4 Stir in the stem ginger, then pour the jam into hot, sterilized jars (see page 8) and seal (see page 11).

green tomato & angelica jam

I came across this combination in *Tomatoes and How to Grow Them* by F. R. Castle, dated 1938. Angelica is an interesting herb to grow and makes a towering plant showy enough to work in the herbaceous border. If you don't have fresh angelica, you may be able to buy candied stems.

Use 50 g/2 oz. fresh stems or 30 g/1¼ oz. candied pieces and follow the recipe for Green Tomato Jam, omitting the stem ginger. If using fresh angelica, choose young stems, pour boiling water over them and allow to steep for 5 minutes before draining and shredding finely. Add to the tomatoes at the beginning. For candied stems, chop finely and add at the end of the recipe instead of the stem ginger.

Makes about 1.65 kg/5¼ cups
250 g/9 oz. blackcurrants
250 g/9 oz. redcurrants
250 g/9 oz. strawberries
250 g/9 oz. raspberries
1 kg/5 cups warmed sugar (see page 10)

tutti frutti jam

Mixed-fruit jams are a good way of using up small amounts of fruits that aren't in a great enough quantity to make jam on their own. You can also combine fruits with lower pectin levels with others that have a higher pectin content, which is an ideal way of helping the jam to set.

1 Strip the black and redcurrants from their stalks by running the tines of a fork through the stems. Place the currants in a preserving pan with enough water just to stop the fruits catching on the bottom of the pan. Bring to the boil, then simmer for 15–20 minutes.

2 Add the strawberries and raspberries and simmer for a further 10 minutes. Add the warmed sugar to the fruit and stir over a low heat until all the sugar has dissolved. Turn up the heat and boil rapidly to reach setting point (see page 10). Skim if necessary (see page 11).

3 Pour the jam into hot, sterilized jars (see page 8) and seal (see page 11).

Makes about 1.3 kg/3¾ cups
1 kg/2 lb. 4 oz. gooseberries, topped
and tailed

800 g/4 cups sugar
juice of 2 lemons

gooseberry jam

Gooseberries make a sharp jam that works equally well as a sweet or savoury accompaniment. The first varieties, ready to pick in early summer, herald the beginning of a season of luscious fruits and their tartness makes them ideal for jam making. Later varieties get sweeter and can be eaten raw.

1 Place all the ingredients in a preserving pan and heat gently until simmering. Remove immediately from the heat and pour the contents into a ceramic or glass bowl. Cover the surface with parchment paper, pushing it down onto the fruit. Leave the bowl overnight in the refrigerator.

2 The next day, pour the contents of the bowl back into the preserving pan and heat gently, stirring to be sure that all the sugar has dissolved. Then turn up the heat and boil rapidly to reach setting point (see page 10). This takes very little time to achieve – only 5–10 minutes – and you need to watch that the syrup doesn't burn. Skim if necessary (see page 11).

3 Pour the jam into hot, sterilized jars (see page 8) and seal (see page 11).

Makes about 1.3 kg/3¾ cups
good handful of fresh elderflowers
1 kg/2 lb. 4 oz. gooseberries, topped
and tailed

800 g/4 cups sugar
juice of 2 lemons

gooseberry & elderflower jam

How convenient that elderflowers are in season at the same time as early gooseberries! Here, again, elderflowers bring their unique and delicate flavour to a classic pairing.

First, shake the flowers, face down, to remove any unwanted creatures, then wrap them in a piece of muslin/cheesecloth and tie into a bundle. Follow the recipe for Gooseberry Jam, pushing the elderflower bundle in among the gooseberries during their initial simmer and when being left to macerate overnight. Remove the bundle before the fruit is returned to the preserving pan for the final cooking time.

Makes about 1.35 kg/4 cups
500 g/1 lb. 2 oz. peaches, quartered
  and stoned/pitted
500 g/1 lb. 2 oz. pears, quartered
juice of 1 lemon
850 g/4¼ cups sugar

peach & pear jam

This is another beautiful combination of delicate flavours. Here I have used a food mill to process the fruits, as I like the texture this method gives to the jam and it cuts down on the initial preparation. You can, however, leave the fruits in whole chunks if you prefer, in which case you will need to peel and core the pears and skin and stone/pit the peaches first.

1 Place the fruit in a pan with the lemon juice plus 1 tablespoon water and heat gently to release the juices and soften the fruit. Simmer for 10 minutes, then remove from the heat and leave to cool.

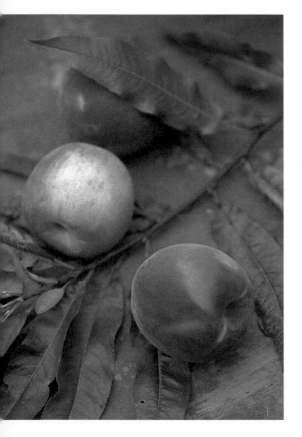

2 Press the fruit mixture through the fine disc of a food mill or a sieve/strainer and collect the puréed pulp in a preserving pan. Add the sugar to the fruit and stir over a low heat until all the sugar has dissolved, then turn up the heat and boil rapidly to reach setting point (see page 10). Skim if necessary (see page 11).

3 Pour the jam into hot, sterilized jars (see page 8) and seal (see page 11).

Makes about 2.1 kg/6 cups

500 g/1 lb. 2 oz. cooking apples,
  roughly chopped
500 g/1 lb. 2 oz. pears, roughly chopped
500 g/1 lb. 2 oz. plums, halved
zest and juice of 1 lemon
25 g/1 oz. root ginger, bruised
2 cloves
1.25 kg/6¼ cups sugar

dumpsideary jam

Dumpsideary jam comes with an endearing name that smacks of tradition and uses a sumptuous medley of orchard fruits – apples, pears and plums – that are in season together. Lightly spiced with ginger and cloves, it is sometimes known as High Dumpsideary while a similar jam without the spices is called Mixty Maxty. When you give a jar of this jam to someone, the name alone is sure to be a talking point.

1 Place all the fruits and the plum stones in a preserving pan along with 300 ml/1¼ cups water and simmer gently until soft.

2 Remove the plum stones/pits, then press all the fruit through the fine disc of a food mill or a sieve/strainer.

3 Place the resulting fruit purée in a preserving pan and add the lemon zest and juice. Tie the spices in a piece of muslin/cheesecloth and add this to the pan along with the sugar. Heat the mixture slowly, stirring until the sugar has completely dissolved. Turn up the heat and boil rapidly to reach setting point (see page 10). Skim if necessary (see page 11).

4 Remove the bundle of spices. Pour the jam pour into hot, sterilized jars (see page 8) and seal (see page 11).

jellies

Made from the juices extracted from the fruit, jellies have a clarity and purity that is very attractive. From the gentle amber hues of crab apple to the glorious ruby shades of raspberry and redcurrant and the density of blackberry jellies, when you hold the jar up to the light it is like gazing through stained glass.

For quantity, see page 12
1 kg/2 lb. 4 oz. blackcurrants
juice of 1 lemon (optional)
warmed sugar (see page 10; for quantity
   see step 5)

blackcurrant jelly

This jelly is deep black and glassy, with a perfectly balanced rich, yet tart, flavour. Blackcurrants have an unmistakable and robust taste that makes them ideal for jams and jellies. (If you prefer a slightly less tart version you can omit the lemon juice.) This one is especially suitable for anyone who prefers a smooth, 'no bits' spread; it is great on toast for breakfast and also makes an excellent filling for a sandwich cake.

1 Strip the blackcurrants from their stalks by running the tines of a fork through their stems.

2 Place the currants in a preserving pan with the lemon juice, if using, and 600 ml/2½ cups water and simmer for 5 minutes until the currants start to burst and the juice flows. Remove from the heat and squash the currants with a fork.

3 Pour the currants and liquid into a jelly bag suspended over a bowl and leave it to drip for several hours or overnight (resisting the urge to help things along by squeezing the bag).

4 As blackcurrants have a high pectin content (see page 7), you can then increase the yield by tipping the pulp back into the preserving pan, along with 300 ml/1¼ cups water, and boiling it for 5 minutes. Pour the pulp back into the jelly bag and leave it to drain for a few hours to extract the juice, collecting it in a measuring jug/pitcher.

5 Allow 450 g/2¼ cups sugar for every 600 ml/2½ cups juice.

6 Heat the juice in a preserving pan over a low heat, then add the warmed sugar. Stir until the sugar has completely dissolved, then turn up the heat and boil rapidly until setting point is reached (see page 10). Skim if necessary (see page 11). Pour into hot, sterilized jars (see page 8) and seal (see page 11).

redcurrant & gooseberry jelly

Gooseberries are almost top of the list for pectin content with redcurrants not too far behind, so you can expect your jelly to have a good set. The redcurrants help to give this jelly a good colour, which the gooseberries alone don't have.

Follow the recipe for Blackcurrant Jelly, but use 500 g/1 lb. 2 oz. each of redcurrants and gooseberries and 400 ml/scant 1¾ cups water. Boil the currants and berries together until soft and bursting, then pour into a jelly bag and collect the juice in a jug/pitcher. Don't boil the fruit pulp for a second time. Complete the jelly as before.

For quantity, see page 12
500 g/1 lb. 2 oz. rosehips, stalks removed
1 kg/2 lb. 4 oz. cooking or tart apples,
   roughly chopped
warmed sugar (see page 10; for quantity
   see step 2)

rosehip jelly

Though not instantly obvious, the juice from these wild berries is rich in vitamin C and has a fantastic flavour. As these fruits are stuffed full of tiny seeds and short itching hairs that are completely inedible, it is necessary to extract the juice from the hips first. This does make rosehips particularly well suited to jelly-making, as cooking them first and pouring through a jelly bag leaves all the unwanted pulp behind.

1 Place the rosehips and the apples in a preserving pan. Add enough water to cover them and simmer gently for around 45 minutes until the fruit is soft and pulpy. Mash the fruit with the back of a spoon, then pour it into a jelly bag and leave undisturbed overnight, collecting the drips underneath in a measuring jug/pitcher.

2 Allow 450 g/2¼ cups sugar for every 600 ml/2½ cups juice. Place the juice in a preserving pan, add the warmed sugar and stir over a low heat until all the sugar has dissolved, then turn up the heat and boil rapidly to reach setting point (see page 10). Skim if necessary (see page 11).

3 Pour the jelly into hot, sterilized jars (see page 8) and seal (see page 11).

rowan jelly

Rowan berries come from the European mountain ash tree and make a well-set jelly, with their slightly bitter flavour offset by apples or quinces. Serve as an accompaniment to venison, grouse and hare.

Use equal amounts of rowan berries and apples, or quinces if you have some, for this jelly. Make it in the same way as the Rosehip Jelly. As this preserve is often served with rich meats, adding chopped rosemary to the jelly before potting works well, although it is inclined to settle at the bottom of the jars.

For quantity, see page 12
1 kg/2 lb. 4 oz. crab apples, roughly chopped
sugar (for quantity see step 4)

crab apple jelly

Crab apples seem like such a neglected fruit, yet in season they are often abundant. Their small size makes them far too fiddly for peeling and coring, so you either make them into jelly or purée the fruit for curds, fruit butters or pie fillings. When making jelly, the aim is to end up with something that is as clear as can be.

Different apples will produce jellies in different shades, from amber through to rose, and they always look beautiful when the light shines through them. For a spicier version, you can add a few cloves, a cinnamon stick or some slices of root ginger to the fruit when it is being cooked at the beginning, although I much prefer the single flavour of the fruit to sing through.

1 Place the crab apples in a preserving pan with 500 ml/ 2 cups water. Simmer for about 45 minutes until the fruits have softened and turned fluffy, mashing them with a wooden spoon.

2 Place the apples in a jelly bag suspended over a measuring jug/pitcher to catch the drips. Allow the apples to drain naturally for several hours or overnight – don't be tempted to squeeze the bag if you want your jelly to be beautifully clear.

3 To extract more juice, remove the pulp from the bag, place in a pan with 300 ml/1¼ cups water and bring it to the boil again. Return it to the bag and allow to drain again for a few hours.

4 Allow 450 g/2¼ cups sugar for every 600 ml/2½ cups juice. Add the sugar to the juice, stirring over a low heat until the sugar has completely dissolved. Turn up the heat and boil rapidly to reach setting point (see page 10).

5 Skim if necessary (see page 11). Pour the jelly into hot, sterilized jars (see page 8) and seal (see page 11).

For quantity, see page 12
500 g/1 lb. 2 oz. apples
500 g/1 lb. 2 oz damsons
sugar (for quantity see step 4 of Crab
  Apple Jelly)

damson & apple jelly

Making damsons into jelly is the perfect solution to the 'stoning/pitting the fruit' dilemma – the most tedious aspect of this fruit. Let the jelly bag do the work for you.

Follow the instructions for Crab Apple Jelly, first cooking the apples in 500 ml/2 cups water and adding the damsons for the final 15 minutes. Pour the mixed fruits into a jelly bag and complete as before.

For quantity, see page 12
500 g/1 lb. 2 oz. apples
500 g/1 lb. 2 oz. sloes
sugar (for quantity see step 4 of Crab
  Apple Jelly)

sloe & apple jelly

Sloes added to an apple jelly give it an exquisite rosy hue and a lovely tart taste. This is another versatile preserve, which works with both sweet and savoury things and can be served with meats and cheeses. Sloes are supposed to be best picked after the first frost and can be found by foraging in the hedgerows.

Follow the instructions for Crab Apple Jelly, first cooking the apples in 500 ml/ 2 cups water, then adding the sloes during the last 15 minutes of cooking time. Pour everything into a jelly bag and complete as before.

For quantity, see page 12
1.4 kg/3 lb. 2 oz. blackberries
juice of ½ lemon
sugar (for quantity see step 3)

bramble jelly

Children seem to love collecting blackberries, so put them to work gathering the fruit for this jelly. Often bramble jelly has added spices but I much prefer the real fruit taste to dominate so here I have opted for the pure fruit with just a hint of lemon to help it set.

1 Place the berries in a preserving pan with 100 ml/ 7 tablespoons water. Simmer the fruit for 5 minutes until soft, mashing the berries with a wooden spoon.

2 Pour the fruit into a jelly bag, suspended over a measuring jug/pitcher to catch the drips, and leave for several hours or overnight until the pulp left in the bag is almost dry.

3 Allow 450 g/2¼ cups sugar for every 600 ml/2½ cups juice. Add the lemon juice to the blackberry juice and pour into a preserving pan. Add the sugar and stir over a gentle heat until it is completely dissolved, then turn up the heat and boil rapidly to reach setting point (see page 10).

4 Skim if necessary (see page 11). Pour the jelly into hot, sterilized jars (see page 8) and seal (see page 11).

raspberry jelly

This jelly is the most wondrous, jewel-like colour and is superbly fruity, making it ideal for using as the filling in a sponge cake. It also suits anyone who hates seeds in their preserves.

Follow the instructions for Bramble Jelly, substituting raspberries for the blackberries.

marmalades

'Marmalade' usually refers to a preserve made from citrus fruits, served with toast at breakfast. Bitter Seville oranges make the best traditional citrus marmalade. However, the first marmalade was made from quinces and had Portuguese origins, while in France marmalade is made from other puréed fruits.

Makes about 1.3 kg/4 cups
500 g/1 lb. 2 oz. blackcurrants
500 g/1 lb. 2 oz. apples, cut into large chunks
warmed sugar (see page 10; for quantity see
   step 3)

apple & blackcurrant marmalade

Although this marmalade doesn't contain any citrus fruits, the blackcurrants give just the right amount of tartness and punch to make it a perfect preserve for serving at breakfast. Processing the fruits through a food mill makes the most use of the fruit with very little preparation: there is no need to peel and core the apples at the beginning as the food mill separates these from the flesh later to leave a purée that still has some texture to it.

As is often the case, when there are apples available, there is usually an abundant supply, and this is another great way of finding a use for an apple glut. Windfalls will do the job nicely, as this recipe doesn't call for the most perfect specimens.

1 Strip the blackcurrants from their stalks by running the tines of a fork through the stems.

2 Place all the fruit together in a pan with 3 tablespoons water (just enough to keep the fruit from catching on the bottom of the pan). Simmer gently until the fruit is soft, the juices flow and the apples are fluffy. Remove from the heat and leave until cool enough to handle.

3 Press the fruit mixture through the fine disc of a food mill or a sieve/strainer into a bowl. Weigh the purée, then pour it into a preserving pan and add an equal weight of warmed sugar. Stir over a low heat until all the sugar has dissolved, then turn up the heat and boil rapidly to reach setting point (see page 10). Skim if necessary (see page 11).

4 Pour the marmalade into hot, sterilized jars (see page 8) and seal (see page 11).

apple & cranberry marmalade

This is a variation on the previous recipe and it illustrates the supreme versatility of apples and how they will blend with just about any fruit. Using this template, you can combine whatever fruits you have a plentiful supply of, half and half with apples, cook and process to a purée, then match the weight in sugar. Make this marmalade using crab apples or varieties of cooking apple with a sharp flavour and offset them with another tangy fruit.

Follow the recipe for Apple & Blackcurrant Marmalade, substituting cranberries for the blackcurrants.

Makes about 2 kg/6 cups
1 kg/2 lb. 4 oz. Seville oranges

1 lemon
1.5 kg/7½ cups sugar

seville orange marmalade

Seville oranges are available only for a short time in late winter, but they do make the best marmalade, which makes finding them worth the effort. Because of their extremely bitter taste, they are used only for cooking, but it is this robust quality that makes them particularly good when cooked and sweetened. You are either a cut-rind person or a smooth marmalade person, but shreds of perfectly cooked sweetened rind suspended in this amber jelly get my vote any day.

1 Preheat the oven to 160°C fan/180°C/350°F/Gas 4. Place the whole fruits in a heavy, lidded casserole/Dutch oven or a preserving pan that will fit in the oven. Pour in 1.25 litres/5 cups water and bring it to simmering point on the hob/stovetop.

2 Cover the pan (if using a preserving pan, make a lid from kitchen foil) and place in the oven. Poach the fruit for 2½–3 hours, by which time the skins will be soft.

3 Using a spoon, lift the fruit out of the liquid into a colander. When cool enough to handle, cut each fruit in half and scoop out the pulp with a spoon, leaving just the peel, placing the pulp, pith and pips, in a muslin/cheesecloth bag suspended over a bowl to catch any drips. (Alternatively, use a large piece of muslin gathered into a bag and tied with string.) Measure the liquid, adding any collected in the bowl under the drained pulp, and if necessary add water to make it up to 1 litre/4 cups.

4 Place the muslin bag in a saucepan with enough poaching liquid to cover. Bring to the boil and simmer for 15 minutes. Leave until cool enough to handle, then squeeze the bag to get as much of the liquid as possible from the pulp. Discard the bag and its contents.

5 Chop the rind into thin strips and put into a preserving pan. Add all the poaching liquid. If the mixture is cold, you can add the sugar without warming it; otherwise you will need to warm the sugar first (see page 10). Stir the sugar into the orange liquid over a low heat until completely dissolved and the liquid is clear, then boil rapidly for 15 minutes and test for setting point (see page 10).

6 Turn off the heat and leave the marmalade to stand for 15 minutes, then stir to distribute the peel. Skim if necessary (see page 11). Pour into hot, sterilized jars (see page 8) and seal (see page 11).

Makes about 1.5 kg/5 cups
450 g/1 lb. dried figs

3 lemons
1.1 kg/2 lb. 7 oz. warmed sugar (see page 10)

lemon & fig marmalade

This unusual combination is well worth trying. The lemon half-moons are left in large chunks which give a lovely candied tang to the preserve. Along with the figs, they make a great start to the day.

1 Remove the stalks from the figs and cut each into 4 chunks. Halve the lemons lengthways, then slice the halves thinly, collecting all the juice and any pips. Place the pips in a piece of muslin/cheesecloth and tie it into a bag with string. Place the lemon slices and juice, the figs and the wrapped pips in a large bowl, cover them with 1.1 litres/4½ cups water and leave for 24 hours.

2 Pour the mixture into a pan and heat to simmering; leave simmering for 1–1½ hours until the lemon rind is soft. Leave to cool slightly and remove the pips.

3 Add the warmed sugar. Stir over a low heat, without boiling, until the sugar has completely dissolved, then bring the marmalade to a rapid boil and cook until it reaches setting point (see page 10). Skim if necessary (see page 11). Pot into hot, sterilized jars (see page 8) and seal (see page 11).

Makes about 1 kg/3¼ cups
juice and pared rind of 12 limes
680 g/1 lb. 8 oz. warmed sugar (see page 10)

lime marmalade

If you fancy a change from traditional orange marmalade, then this is the recipe to try. Here is another useful marmalade that can be made at any time of year using shop-bought fruit. It has a great colour and flavour.

Shred the rind pieces finely. Place the pith and pips from the limes in a piece of muslin/cheesecloth and tie it up with string. Put the lime rind and juice and 1.7 litres/7¼ cups water into a preserving pan and bring to the boil, then simmer for 1 hour until the rind is soft. Add the warmed sugar and stir over a low heat until all the sugar has dissolved, then turn up the heat and boil rapidly to reach setting point (see page 10). Remove the muslin bag, then pot up.

Makes about 1.3 kg/4 cups
900 g/2 lb. peaches, roughly chopped
750 g/3¾ cups sugar

peach marmalade

I usually choose a tangy citrus preserve to spread on my toast at breakfast, but this aromatic, slightly gentler marmalade makes a lovely start to the day. You can, of course, eat it just about any time, but it has become one of my morning favourites. The cooking brings out the superb aroma of the fruit – and you could add some vanilla for an even more sybaritic experience.

1 Place the peaches and their stones/pits in a pan along with 250 ml/1 cup water. Bring them to simmering point and simmer until the peach pieces are soft.

2 Discard the stones/pits and press the flesh through the fine disc of a food mill or a sieve/strainer, to give a purée.

3 Put the purée into a preserving pan, add the sugar, warmed if necessary (see step 5, page 65) and stir gently over a low heat until the sugar has completely dissolved. Turn up the heat and boil until it reaches setting point (see page 10). Skim if necessary (see page 11).

4 Pour the marmalade into hot, sterilized jars (see page 8) and seal (see page 11).

peach & vanilla marmalade

Vanilla adds an unmistakable flavour to this breakfast classic. Peaches are wonderfully fragrant anyway, so with added vanilla become positively heavenly. The sticky black seeds scraped from the vanilla pod/bean disperse throughout the preserve. Although called marmalade, it would be a shame to think it can only be eaten for breakfast. This one's a good all rounder.

Split a vanilla pod/bean lengthways and add it to the peaches when cooking them with the water, as above. Remove the pod before puréeing the fruit and scrape the seeds from the pod pieces, using the sharp point of a knife. Stir the seeds into the peach purée and discard the pod pieces. Continue as above.

Makes about 1.5 kg/4¼ cups
1 kg/2 lb. 4 oz. quinces, fur washed off
3 oranges

warmed sugar (see page 10; for quantity
see step 5)

quince & orange marmalade

Reputedly, the original marmalade was a preserve made from quinces, and the name comes from the word *marmelo*, the Portuguese word for this fruit. Quince seems to be a long-forgotten fruit, not often found for sale, though you may come across it in Mediterranean food stores. If you have a quince tree, use these wonderful fruits with orange to make a delicious marmalade. The quinces are cooked very slowly to intensify their flavour and bring out the best in them – use the oven on the lowest setting or cook the marmalade in a slow cooker for a similar result.

1 Place the fruits in a lidded casserole dish/Dutch oven (use a second casserole if they won't all fit into one) and pour in enough boiling water to cover the fruits so they just begin to float. Put on the lid and slow cook in the oven at its lowest setting for 6–8 hours or overnight, or cook in a slow cooker or crock-pot.

2 Remove from the oven and leave until cool enough to handle. Strain the liquid through a colander into a pan. Peel the quinces, quarter them and remove the cores, then place the skins and cores in with the cooking liquid. Cut 2 of the oranges in half, scoop out the flesh and add the pips and pith to the liquid as well. Put the peel to one side.

3 Bring the mixture to the boil and reduce it down to about a third or a half of the original quantity. Pour the reduced mixture through a sieve/strainer into a preserving pan.

4 Cut the quinces into chunky slices about 2-cm/¾-inch square and 1-cm/½-inch thick. Slice the whole orange into thin rounds and chop the empty orange halves into fine shreds.

5 Weigh the quince, orange slices and shredded rind, add them to the reduced mixture and warm through. Add the same weight of warmed sugar and stir over a low heat until all the sugar has dissolved, taking care to keep the orange slices intact, then turn up the heat and boil rapidly to reach setting point (see page 10). Skim if necessary (see page 11).

6 Remove the orange slices with a slotted spoon and use them to decorate the insides of the hot, sterilized jars (see page 8) by standing them on end against the glass. Pour the marmalade into the jars and seal (see page 11).

curds

These little pots of fruity loveliness are totally delicious. I make a selection of curds and serve them in teaspoon-sized dollops in bite-sized sweet pastry cases. Each one can be savoured, discussed and relished with due ceremony. Fruit curds don't keep quite so well as jams, but they won't hang around long enough anyway.

Makes about 900 g/3 cups
1 vanilla pod/bean
600 g/1 lb. 5 oz. crab apples, halved, or
   cooking apples, cut roughly into chunks

115 g/½ cup butter, preferably unsalted,
   cut into cubes
450 g/2¼ cups caster/granulated sugar
3 large (UK)/extra large (US) eggs, plus
   2 egg yolks, beaten

crab apple & vanilla curd

Crab apples have just the right amount of tartness to give this curd lots of flavour, but any sharp apples will do the job just as well. Because the fruit is puréed, there isn't much preparation needed, so windfalls can be used, if desired, more or less as they are (just with any bad bits removed). This curd makes the most fabulous filling for a sweet pastry case.

1 Split the vanilla pod/bean lengthways and place it with the apples in a pan, adding 1 tablespoon water. Simmer gently until the apples are soft, stirring occasionally to be sure the fruit doesn't catch on the bottom of the pan. Remove it from the heat and leave to cool.

2 Remove the vanilla pod, then purée the apples by pressing them through the fine disc of a food mill or a sieve/strainer collecting the resulting purée in a bowl. Scrape the seeds from the vanilla pod pieces with a sharp knife and add them to the apples along with the pod. Add the other ingredients, pouring the egg through a sieve.

3 Place the bowl over a pan of simmering water (or use a double boiler) and heat gently, stirring all the time until everything is blended and the curd begins to thicken and coats the back of the spoon. This stage should take about 20–30 minutes.

4 Remove the vanilla pod pieces. Pour the hot curd into small, hot, sterilized jars (see page 8) and seal (see page 11).

Makes about 500 g/1½ cups
225 g/8 oz. apricots, quartered and stoned
2 large (UK)/extra large (US) eggs, well
    beaten
zest and juice of 1 lemon

50 g/3½ tablespoons butter, preferably
    unsalted, cut into cubes
225 g/1 cup pus 2 tablespoons caster/
    granulated sugar

apricot curd

Fresh home-grown apricots cannot be bettered, but even a punnet-full from the supermarket will make tasty curd. Choose the best-quality organic eggs when making curds as they also help to give a brighter colour to the finished product.

1 Place the apricots in a pan with 2 tablespoons water (just enough to stop the fruit from catching on the bottom of the pan) and cook gently until soft.

2 Cool the fruit slightly, then press it through the fine disc of a food mill or a sieve/strainer, collecting the resulting purée in a bowl.

3 Strain the beaten eggs through a sieve/strrainer into the purée. Add the lemon zest and juice, the butter and the sugar.

4 Place the bowl over a pan of simmering water (or use a double boiler). Cook gently, stirring continuously with a wooden spoon, until the mixture is completely blended and thickens enough to coat the back of the spoon. This should take about 30 minutes.

5 Pour the curd into small, hot, sterilized jars (see page 8) and seal (see page 11).

Makes about 350 g/1 cup
250 g/9 oz. raspberries
170 g/¾ cup plus 2 tablespoons
 caster/granulated sugar

50 g/3½ tablespoons butter, preferably
 unsalted, cut into cubes
2 large (UK)/extra large (US) eggs, beaten

raspberry curd

Raspberries give this delicious curd a wonderful colour and a lovely tangy taste. Save small unusual-shaped glass jars especially for potting up curds. They are great to give as presents.

1 Place the raspberries in a pan and cook gently for 5–10 minutes, squashing the fruits with a spoon to help release the juice.

2 Push the fruit through a sieve/strainer, collecting the purée in a bowl.

3 Place the bowl over a pan of simmering water (or use a double boiler) and add all the other ingredients, pouring the beaten eggs through a sieve/strainer onto the purée. Stir with a wooden spoon until everything is well blended. Continue cooking, stirring constantly, until the curd is thick enough to coat the back of the spoon – this should take about 20–30 minutes.

4 Pour the curd into small, hot, sterilized jars (see page 8) and seal (see page 11).

Makes about 450 g/2 cups
225 g/8 oz. blueberries
zest and juice of 1 lime
2 large (UK)/extra large (US) eggs, beaten

50 g/3½ tablespoons butter, preferably
 unsalted, cut into cubes
225 g/1 cup plus 2 tablespoons caster/
 granulated sugar

blueberry & lime curd

The best and tastiest blueberries err on the tart side and here these berries benefit from an added boost with the addition of the zest and juice of a lime.

Place the blueberries in a pan with the lime zest and juice and cook gently for 5–10 minutes until tender. Purée the fruit and continue as for steps 2–4 of Raspberry Curd.

Makes about 450 g/2 cups

450 g/1 lb. gooseberries, any large
   stems removed
zest of 1 lime
100 g/7 tablespoons butter, preferably
   unsalted, cut into cubes
200 g/1 cup caster/granulated sugar
3 large (UK)/extra large (US) eggs
   plus 2 yolks, beaten

gooseberry curd

This curd isn't one you are likely to find for sale anywhere, so you have no option but to make it yourself at home. Gooseberries are relatively easy to grow and don't need much attention to flourish so it is well worth growing some just to make this curd.

1 Place the gooseberries in a pan with 85 ml/6 tablespoons water and cook gently for 5–10 minutes, squashing the fruits with a spoon to help release the juice.

2 Press the fruit through the fine disc of a food mill or a sieve/strainer, to remove the skins and seeds, collecting the purée in a bowl.

3 Place the bowl over a pan of simmering water (or use a double boiler) and add all the other ingredients, pouring the beaten eggs through a sieve/strainer onto the purée. Continue stirring with a wooden spoon until everything becomes well blended and smooth and thick enough to coat the back of the spoon – this should take about 20–30 minutes.

4 Pour the curd into hot, sterilized jars (see page 8) and seal (see page 11).

Makes about 400 g/1¼ cups
zest and juice of 3 lemons
85 g/6 tablespoons butter, preferably
  unsalted, cut into cubes

200 g/1 cup caster/granulated sugar
3 large (UK)/extra large (US) eggs, beaten

lemon curd

An outstanding classic, this sharp lemon curd makes the perfect filling for an open tart, can be used to sandwich a sponge cake, spread on freshly-baked bread or swirled through vanilla ice cream. Utter perfection, whichever way you serve it.

1 Place the lemon zest and juice in a bowl set over a pan of simmering water (or use a double boiler) along with the butter and sugar. Add the beaten eggs, pouring them through a sieve/strainer

2 Stir with a wooden spoon until everything becomes heated through and well blended. Continue cooking, stirring constantly, until the curd thickens enough to coat the back of the spoon – this should take about 15–20 minutes.

3 Pour the curd into small, hot, sterilized jars (see page 8) and seal (see page 11).

Makes about 350 g/1 cup
zest and juice of 3 Seville oranges
50 g/3½ tablespoons butter, preferably
  unsalted, cut into cubes

170 g/¾ cup plus 2 tablespoons
  caster/granulated sugar
2 large (UK)/extra large (US) eggs, beaten

bitter orange curd

The bitter nature of Seville oranges works perfectly for a curd. Most sweet oranges just don't have enough character to use in this way, although blood oranges have more of a flavour kick than other sweet varieties, so they work well also. Use the curd as a filling for a sweet pastry tart, or spread it liberally to sandwich the layers of a rich chocolate cake, or simply serve it on a thick slice of fresh bread.

Follow the instructions for making Lemon Curd using the ingredients above.

Makes about 400 g/1¼ cups
zest of 2 small grapefruit
6 tablespoons grapefruit juice

85 g/6 tablespoons butter, preferably
  unsalted, cut into cubes
200 g/1 cup caster/granulated sugar
3 large (UK)/extra large (US) eggs, beaten

grapefruit curd

Here's another citrus variation on the lemon curd theme. This curd is smooth and creamy but still has its own distinct tang.

Follow the instructions for making Lemon Curd using the ingredients above.

Makes about 1.4 kg/1½ cups

1 small butternut squash, peeled, deseeded and
    roughly chopped
zest and juice of 1 lemon
zest and juice of 1 orange
70 g/5 tablespoons butter, preferably unsalted,
    cut into cubes
200 g/1 cup caster/granulated sugar
2 large (UK)/extra large (US) eggs, plus 2 yolks, beaten
4 pieces of stem ginger (about 75 g/2¾ oz.), finely
    chopped
3 tablespoons syrup from the stem ginger

butternut & ginger curd

Squashes and pumpkins are naturally sweet so can be made into sweet preserves really well.
Here butternut squash is the main ingredient, but other types can be used instead. The brighter
orange the flesh, the better. Chopped pieces of stem ginger add a lovely bite to the texture.

1 Place the squash in a pan with 100 ml/7 tablespoons
water to stop it from sticking to the pan as it cooks. Cover
and cook until soft, then pour off any excess liquid.

2 Purée the squash in a food processor or pass it through
the fine disc of a food mill. Alternatively, press it through
a sieve/strainer.

3 Measure out 300 g/1½ cups of the squash purée and
place this in a bowl over simmering water (or use a double
boiler), along with all the other ingredients, pouring the
beaten eggs through a sieve/strainer onto the purée.
Continue stirring with a wooden spoon until everything
becomes well blended, the sugar is dissolved and the curd
thickens and will coat the back of the spoon – this should
take about 30 minutes.

4 Pour the curd into small, hot, sterilized jars (see page 8)
and seal (see page 11).

cordials

Cordials, nectars and syrups are, in fact, the same thing. These sweetened fruity concentrates are delicious diluted with water, added to milk for milk shakes, poured over ice cream or swirled through cake batter prior to baking for a marbled effect. At best they really capture the essence of the fruit. Use over-ripe fruit for best results.

Makes about 750 ml/3 cups
900 g/2 lb. over-ripe blackcurrants
sugar (for quantity see step 3)

blackcurrant cordial

Rich in vitamin C, blackcurrants are an ideal fruit for making into cordials that can then be diluted either as a cold drink or a hot comforting drink. The homemade version knocks spots off anything you will find for sale.

1 Strip the blackcurrants from their stalks by running the tines of a fork through the stems.

2 Place them with 400 ml/1¾ cups water in the top of a double boiler or in a bowl over a pan of simmering water and cook for half an hour, stirring occasionally and mashing the fruit with the back of the spoon, then strain through a sieve/strainer into a measuring jug/pitcher and discard the pulp.

3 Add 450 g/2¼ cups sugar to every 600 ml/2½ cups juice and stir over a low heat until all the sugar has dissolved. Bring just to the boil, then remove quickly from the heat.

4 Pour the cordial into clean clip-top or corked bottles and sterilize (see page 14), or pour into freezer containers, seal and freeze.

damson cordial

Made into a cordial, freshly picked damsons make a sublime and unusual cordial bursting with tart flavour. Drizzle over yogurt or ice cream.

Follow the recipe for Blackcurrant Cordial, substituting damsons for the blackcurrants.

Makes about 1.5 litres/6½ cups
20 heads of elderflower
1.5 kg/7½ cups sugar
40 g/1½ oz. citric acid
2 lemons, thinly sliced
2 oranges, thinly sliced

elderflower cordial

The shrubby elder (*Sambucus nigra*) is so common in the countryside that it is easy to pass it by without a second look. Yet in early summer it provides one of the most distinctive ingredients of the preserving year – one that can be foraged for free. The heavily scented blossoms make a refreshing cordial that you can dilute with still or sparkling mineral water. The fragrance, as well as the taste, evokes lazy summer afternoons. Gather the flower heads on dry, sunny days, away from busy roads, and select flower heads that are fresh and white, avoiding older creamy-yellow blossoms. This delicious cordial will keep for around 2 months in the fridge; if frozen in plastic containers, it will last for a year or more – so be sure to make plenty.

1 Shake the flowers, face down, to remove any unwanted creatures.

2 Place the sugar and 1.2 litres/ 5 cups water in a stainless steel or enamel pan and warm slowly, stirring, to dissolve the sugar completely, then bring the resulting syrup to a boil.

3 Add the flowers, bring again to the boil, then remove from the heat.

4 Add the other ingredients, stir well, then leave, covered, in a cool place for 24 hours.

5 Strain the cordial into clean clip-top or corked bottles and sterilize (see page 14).

Makes about 750 ml/3 cups
50 g/2 oz. fresh root ginger, bruised

juice and thinly pared rind of 2 lemons
sugar (for quantity see step 2)

ginger & lemon cordial

This cordial, though not intentionally medicinal, is soothing and warming and is ideal to drink as a hot beverage if you feel a cold coming on.

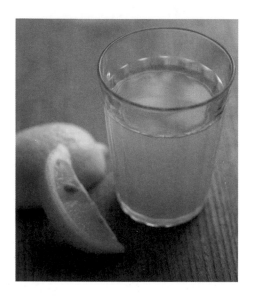

1 Place the ginger and and lemon rind in a pan with 1.2 litres/5 cups water. Simmer gently for 40 minutes. Strain through a sieve/strainer into a measuring jug/pitcher and discard the rind and ginger.

2 Add 400 g/2 cups sugar to every 600 ml/2½ cups liquid and the lemon juice and stir over a low heat until all the sugar has dissolved. Bring just to the boil, then remove quickly from the heat.

3 Pour the cordial into clean clip-top or corked bottles and sterilize (see page 14), or pour into freezer containers, seal and freeze.

Makes about 2 litres/2 quarts
8–10 lemons
6–8 oranges

650 g/3¼ cups sugar
1½ teaspoons citric acid

lemon & orange cordial

A fresh citrus cordial that is so classic and versatile that you can drink it any time. This cordial makes a drink like the best old-fashioned lemonade mixed with orangeade.

Pare the rind finely from 1 lemon and 1 orange. Put the sugar, rind and 600 ml/ 2½ cups water into a pan. Heat gently to make a syrup, then boil for 5 minutes. Strain through a sieve/strainer into a measuring jug/pitcher; discard the rind. Squeeze sufficient lemons and oranges to produce the same amount of juice as syrup, keeping the proportions half lemon, half orange. Mix the syrup and fruit juices together in the pan and add the citric acid, stirring until the powder has dissolved. Bottle as above.

Makes about 600 ml/2½ cups
450 g/1 lb. rosehips, freshly gathered
sugar (for quantity see step 5)

rosehip cordial

Rosehips are one of the most popular foraged fruits, offered for free from nature's larder. They are the fruit of the wild rose, and gathering them is all part of the fun. They should be picked fully ripe, when a deep red colour and preferably after the first frosts, which soften them. If picked a little earlier, you can place them, freshly picked, into the freezer overnight to give the same result as if they had been nipped by the frost. Rosehip cordial has a high vitamin C content and is so sweet and delicious that it is a great way of encouraging children to boost their vitamin intake effortlessly.

1 Place the rosehips in a pan and mash them with the back of a spoon to break them down. Pour 1 litre/4 cups boiling water over them, to cover, and simmer for 5 minutes until the hips are soft.

2 Remove the pan from the heat and leave to stand for 15 minutes, then strain the mixture through a jelly bag, collecting the juice in a measuring jug/pitcher. Set the juice aside.

3 Remove the pulp from the jelly bag and place it in the pan. Add 500 ml/ 2 cups water and bring the mixture to the boil, then repeat step 2, but this time squeezing out the excess liquid from the pulp.

4 Combine both jugs/pitchers of juice in the pan and boil the mixture to reduce it by approximately a third to a half.

5 Add 325 g/1½ cups sugar to every 600 ml/2½ cups juice and stir over a low heat until all the sugar has dissolved. Bring just to the boil, then remove quickly from the heat.

6 Pour the cordial into clean clip-top or corked bottles and sterilize (see page 14), or pour into freezer containers, seal and freeze.

Makes about 600 ml/2½ cups
1 kg/2 lb. 4 oz. over-ripe raspberries
sugar (for quantity see step 2)

raspberry cordial

Raspberry cordial makes a lovely alternative to a dollop of jam on your rice pudding. Unlike preserves, which often benefit from being made with combinations and medleys of flavours, cordials are usually best when made with a single fruit, thus showcasing the individual characteristics of that fruit.

1 Place the raspberries in the top of a double boiler or in a bowl over a pan of simmering water. Mash the berries with the back of a spoon to break them down and add 1 tablespoon water, then cook until the fruit is soft, the juices are flowing and the fruit comes to the boil, stirring now and again. Pour into a jelly bag and collect the drips in a measuring jug/pitcher.

2 Add 400 g/2 cups sugar to every 600 ml/2 cups juice and stir over a low heat until all the sugar has dissolved. Bring just to the boil, then remove quickly from the heat.

3 Pour the cordial into clean clip-top or corked bottles and sterilize (see page 14), or pour into freezer containers, seal and freeze.

Makes about 1.2 litres/5 cups
600 g/3 cups sugar

1 kg/2 lb. 4 oz. over-ripe apricots, halved and stoned/pitted

apricot cordial

Another lush and fruity treat to dilute down into a refreshing summer drink. It is still worth making a smaller quantity even if there aren't many apricots to go around.

Put the sugar and 1.2 litres/5 cups water in a pan and heat gently to make a syrup. Add the apricots to the syrup, simmering until the fruit pieces are tender. Strain through a sieve/strainer into a measuring jug/pitcher (Do not discard the apricots. Instead, use them as a delicious pie filling or serve them with cream.) Pour the cordial into clean clip-top or corked bottles and sterilize (see page 14), or pour into freezer containers, seal and freeze.

strawberry cordial

The vibrant colour and evocative scent of this syrup shouts out summer. Pick your own or choose locally-grown fruit so the berries are at their freshest and sweetest.

Follow the recipe for Raspberry Cordial, substituting strawberries for the raspberries.

Makes about 600 ml/2½ cups
900 g/2 lb. over-ripe blackberries
sugar (for quantity see step 2)

blackberry cordial

An unusual twist for this foraged fruit when topped up with a sparkling white wine or a glug of champagne to make a kir royale with a rustic kick.

1 Place the blackberries with 100 ml/7 tablespoons water in the top of a double boiler or in a bowl over a pan of simmering water. Cook for 1 hour, stirring occasionally and mashing the fruit with the back of the spoon, then strain through a sieve/strainer into a measuring jug/pitcher and discard the pulp.

2 Add 450 g/2¼ cups sugar to every 600 ml/2½ cups juice and stir over a low heat until all the sugar has dissolved. Bring just to the boil, then remove quickly from the heat.

3 Pour the cordial into clean clip-top or corked bottles and sterilize (see page 14), or pour into freezer containers, seal and freeze.

Makes about 600 ml/2½ cups
1 kg/2 lb. 4 oz. over-ripe mulberries
sugar (for quantity see below)

mulberry cordial

Gathering mulberries can be a hazardous occupation. The traditional method involves spreading a sheet on the ground underneath the branches and shaking the tree until the fruit drops.

Place the mulberries in the top of a double boiler or in a bowl over a pan of simmering water. Mash the fruits with the back of a spoon to break them down and add 1 tablespoon water, then cook until the fruit is soft and the juices are flowing and the fruit comes to the boil, stirring now and again. Pour into a jelly bag and collect the drips in a measuring jug/pitcher. Add 400 g/2 cups sugar to every 600 m/2½ cups juice and stir over a low heat until all the sugar has dissolved. Bring just to the boil, then remove quickly from the heat. Bottle as above.

700 g/1 lb. 9 oz. over-ripe redcurrants
3 over-ripe nectarines (approx. 450 g/1 lb.
   in weight), halved, stoned/pitted and diced
sugar (for quantity see step 3)

redcurrant & nectarine cordial

Redcurrants and nectarines make a colourful cordial that tastes great as well. As is the way
with all cordials, you could pour this into ice-lolly moulds and freeze.

1 Strip the redcurrants from their stalks – the simplest and quickest way is
to run the tines of a fork through the stems.

2 Place the nectarines in the top of
a double boiler or in a bowl over a
pan of simmering water. Mash the
fruits with the back of a spoon to
break them down and add 100 ml/
7 tablespoons water. Cook until the
fruit is soft, then add the redcurrants
and continue to cook until they are
soft and the juice is flowing. Strain
through a sieve/strainer into a
measuring jug/pitcher and discard
the pulp.

3 Add 400 g/2 cups sugar to every
600 ml/2½ cups juice and stir over
a low heat until all the sugar has
dissolved. Bring just to the boil, then
remove quickly from the heat.

4 Pour the cordial into clean clip-top
or corked bottles and sterilize (see
page 14), or pour into freezer
containers, seal and freeze.

fruits in syrup

Before the advent of the freezer, bottling fruits and vegetables in water or sugar syrup was the usual way to preserve them. Now that bottling has become a niche activity and freezing the norm, fruits in syrup have taken on an altogether more luxurious feel. Packed in smart jars and spiced or flavoured, they make brilliant presents.

Makes about 750 g/1 lb. 10 oz.
450 g/2¼ cups sugar
pared rind and juice of 1 orange
1 small cinnamon stick

4 cardamom pods, with seeds crushed
2 star anise
750 g/1 lb. 10 oz. apricots, halved and
  stoned/pitted

apricots in syrup

This is a lovely way of using up any luscious apricots that come your way. The syrup is quite spicy and helps make this bottled fruit very special, special enough to serve alone as dessert after dinner. Leaving the whole spices in the jar means it looks good as well.

1 Make a syrup by placing 600 ml/2½ cups water in a pan with the sugar, 3 strips of the orange rind plus the juice of the orange and the spices. Heat gently, stirring to dissolve the sugar before turning up the heat and bringing to a simmer.

2 Add the apricots and poach them until they are cooked but still in whole pieces, then remove them with a slotted spoon and pack them into hot, sterilized jars (see page 8). Bring the syrup to the boil and boil rapidly for 10–15 minutes to thicken and reduce the syrup.

3 Pour the syrup and spices over the fruit to cover completely. Gently tap the jars to release any air bubbles, then seal.

nectarines in syrup

One of summer's most delectable fruits, nectarines also make a special treat when preserved, ready to enjoy in autumn or winter.

Use 750 g/1 lb. 10 oz. nectarines in place of the apricots in Apricots in Syrup. Medium-sized fruits can be used halved with the stones/pits removed, but for larger fruits cut them into quarters and proceed as above.

damsons in syrup

As the damsons are kept whole, you might like to warn anyone eating them to beware of the stones/pits. It is a small price to pay for this delicious preserve.

Use damsons in place of apricots, but keep the fruits whole and poach them gently in the syrup, removing them as soon as you see signs of the skins splitting. Damsons almost always have such a superb flavour that too many spices will only spoil them, so, keep the orange peel and juice but omit the spices from Apricots in Syrup. A darker sugar will also suit this fruit, so use demerara or dark muscovado instead of white sugar.

Fills a 500-ml/17-oz jar
50 g/¼ cup sugar
½ vanilla pod/bean

3-cm/1¼-inch piece of cinnamon stick
6–7 figs, halved
¼ teaspoon citric acid

figs in vanilla syrup

These gorgeous fruits look magnificent in the jar, beautifully pink and jewel-like. Baking the jar in the oven will help the figs to keep for longer.

1 Preheat the oven to 130°C fan/150°C/300°F/Gas 2. Place the sugar, vanilla pod/bean and cinnamon in a pan and add 220 ml/1 scant cup water. Stir over a low heat to dissolve the sugar, then bring to the boil and simmer for 2 minutes to make a syrup. Remove from the heat. Discard the cinnamon stick. Slice the vanilla pod in half lengthways, scrape out the seeds with a knife and add to the syrup.

2 Pack the figs into a clean sterilized jar (see page 8) with the cut sides facing outwards. Push the vanilla pod halves among the figs. Pour the syrup over the figs to fill the jar, swivelling the jar to remove any air bubbles.

3 Wrap kitchen foil over the top of the jar and place it in the oven, on a baking tray lined with several layers of folded newspaper. Bake for 25–30 minutes, by which time the syrup will have turned a lovely shade of pink. Remove from the oven, discard the foil and seal.

Makes about 1 litre/1 quart
6 oranges, cut into 5-mm/¼-inch slices
400 ml/1¾ cups white wine vinegar
300 g/1½ cups sugar

120 g/7 tablespoons clear pale honey
1 small cinnamon stick
2 teaspoons coriander seeds
1 teaspoon whole cloves

orange slices in spiced honey

Using a medley of spices to flavour and honey to sweeten makes a delicious and aromatic syrup.

Place the orange slices in a pan with just enough water to cover. Bring to the boil and simmer for 1 hour until the rind is tender. Strain off the water and discard. Place all other ingredients in a pan and heat gently, stirring, to dissolve the sugar and honey. Add the orange slices and simmer for 30 minutes until the rind is translucent, then pack the slices into sterilized jars (see page 8). Strain the syrup to remove the spices, then return to the pan and boil rapidly for a further 10 minutes to reduce. Pour into the jars to the brim, then seal.

Fills a 1-kg/1-quart wide-necked jar
900 g/2 lb. small peaches (approx. 9 peaches)
300 g/1½ cups sugar
1 vanilla pod/bean (optional)
about 250 ml/1 cup brandy

whole peaches in brandy

Preserving peaches in a brandy syrup is a great way to use up peaches being sold off cheaply at the supermarket. Quite often you find them still firm and perfect, but the date on the packaging turns them into a bargain. Of course if you grow your own peaches, even better! Packed into a jar, they make a wonderful present that looks very impressive. Including a vanilla pod/bean is optional, but it is a resourceful way of using up pods that have already had their seeds removed for other recipes, and they look good showing through the jar. This recipe makes enough to fill one big jar, so adapt quantities if you want to use smaller jars.

1 Skin the peaches by plunging them in boiling water for a couple of minutes. You may need to do this in batches. The skins should peel away easily from the fruits using a sharp knife.

2 Place 400 ml/1 cups water in a pan with half of the sugar and stir over a low heat to dissolve the sugar. Bring the syrup to a simmer and add the vanilla pod/bean, if using.

3 Add the skinned peaches to the syrup, probably in 3 batches, and poach for 5 minutes, spooning the syrup over them if it doesn't cover them. Remove with a slotted spoon and place in a clean sterilized jar, packing them in neatly but taking care not to squash or damage them. Remove the vanilla pod from the syrup and push it down among the fruits.

4 Add the remaining sugar to the syrup in the pan and stir until all the sugar has dissolved, then turn up the heat and boil rapidly for 4 minutes. Remove from the heat and leave to cool for 10 minutes.

5 Measure the syrup, add the same amount of brandy and stir together. Pour the brandy syrup over the peaches to cover, then seal the jar.

greengages in brandy

The greengages have a great colour and aromatic flavour that works really well here. Any brandy left over in the jar after dishing up the fruit can be drunk like a liqueur. Don't waste a drop!

Follow the recipe for Whole Peaches in Brandy, substituting 900 g/2 lb. of firm, ripe greengages for the peaches. There is no need to skin the greengages. Be careful when poaching the fruits that they stay whole, and remove them immediately from the syrup if they show signs of splitting.

Makes about 750 g/1 lb. 10 oz.
450 g/1 lb. ripe cherries
75 g/6 tablespoons sugar
500 ml/2 cups eau de vie

cherries in eau de vie

This has to be the easiest preserve in the book and yet very little effort is rewarded with such a luxurious result. Serve simply with cream and enjoy.

1 Use a cherry stoner to stone/pit the cherries and remove any stalks, then pack them into sterilized, wide-necked jars (see page 8), layering the fruits with sugar now and again. When the jars are filled with cherries, spoon any remaining sugar on top.

2 Pour the eau de vie over the cherries, filling the jars to the top, and seal. Store the jars for at least 6 weeks, giving the jars a shake from time to time to help dissolve the sugar and create a syrup.

chutneys

Chutney making is an inexact science, and you can adjust spices and sweetness to suit your tastes. It requires a long cooking time to reach a rich, thick consistency, but don't cook it until too dry as it will dry out slightly in storage – a shiny, moist chutney is what you are aiming for. You must be patient and leave chutneys to mature before eating.

Makes about 1.3 kg/4¼ cups
1 teaspoon allspice
1 teaspoon mustard seeds
1 teaspoon ground coriander
1 small cinnamon stick
450 g/1 lb. apricots, quartered and
    stoned/pitted
450 g/1 lb. cooking apples, peeled, cored
    and chopped into large chunks

750 ml/3¼ cups cider, wine or white
    malt vinegar
225 g/1½ cups sultanas/golden raisins
    chopped
2 garlic cloves, peeled and chopped
rind and juice of 1 lemon
1 teaspoon salt
2-cm/¾-inch square piece of fresh root
    ginger, peeled and finely chopped
450 g/2¼ cups warmed sugar (see page 10)

apricot chutney

This chutney can be made using either fresh or dried fruit. Here, the recipe uses fresh apricots, making the most of a seasonal glut. However, if you want to make it out of season, you can use dried apricots instead: simply replace the fresh apricots with 300 g/10 oz. dried apricots, soaked for a few hours in the vinegar, then proceed in the same way.

1 Place the spices in a piece of muslin/cheesecloth and tie it into a bag with string. Place the apricots, apples, vinegar and spice bag in a stainless steel preserving pan and bring to the boil, then simmer for 10 minutes.

2 Add the other ingredients and stir over a low heat until all the sugar has dissolved, then bring to the boil and simmer for approximately 1½ hours until the chutney is thick but still juicy, stirring occasionally.

3 Remove the muslin bag, then pour the chutney into hot, sterilized jars (see page 8) and seal (see page 11).

apricot & orange chutney

Orange is a great companion to apricots and helps the chutney to be even more colourful. This recipe is another useful one as it can be made at any time of year using dried apricots.

Replace the lemon in the Apricot Chutney with 3 large oranges. Grate the zest from them and cut away and discard the white pith, then chop the orange flesh roughly. Add them in step 2 and continue as above.

Makes about 2.75 kg/9 cups

900 g/2 lb. raw beetroot/beets, peeled and coarsely grated

450 g/1 lb. onions, peeled and chopped

700 g/1 lb. 9 oz. cooking apples, peeled, cored and chopped

450 g/3 cups seedless raisins

1.1 litres/4½ cups malt vinegar or spiced pickling vinegar (see page 13)

900 g/4½ cups sugar

2 teaspoons ground ginger

beetroot chutney

Beetroots/beets are a vegetable that you can have too many of at the height of the growing season, so chutney-making suits them well.

1 Place everything in a stainless steel preserving pan and stir over a gentle heat to dissolve the sugar. Bring to the boil, then simmer gently for about 1 hour until the beetroot/beets and onions are soft and the chutney is thick but still juicy, stirring occasionally.

2 Pour the chutney into hot, sterilized jars (see page 8) and seal (see page 11).

Makes about 1.5 kg/5¼ cups

400 g/14 oz. courgettes/zucchini

2 teaspoons salt, plus extra for sprinkling

400 g/14 oz. runner/string beans, cut into 2-cm/¾-inch pieces

200 g/1½ cups sweetcorn/corn kernels

450 g/1 lb. onions, finely chopped

600 ml/2½ cups malt or cider vinegar

1 tablespoon cornflour/cornstarch

1 tablespoon English mustard powder

1 tablespoon ground turmeric

1 green chilli/chile, deseeded and finely chopped

350 g/2 cups warmed demerara sugar (see page 10)

vegetable garden chutney

This chutney is a great way of using up homegrown odds and ends, especially useful when produce is growing faster than you can consume it. Try other combinations of vegetables too.

Cut the courgettes/zucchini in half lengthways, then into slices. Place in a bowl and sprinkle with salt, leave for 1 hour, then rinse thoroughly and drain. Place all the vegetables and the vinegar in a stainless steel preserving pan. Bring to the boil, then simmer for 10 minutes. Mix the cornflour/cornstarch, mustard and turmeric in a bowl with a few spoonfuls of vinegar from the pan to form a smooth paste. Add the paste to the pan with the chilli/chile and warmed sugar and stir over a low heat until the sugar has dissolved, then simmer for ¾–1 hour until the chutney is thick but juicy, stirring occasionally. Pot as above.

Makes about 2 kg/6 cups

1 kg/2 lb. 4 oz. damsons
1 litre/1 quart malt vinegar
1 cinnamon stick
1 heaped tablespoon allspice
1 teaspoon cloves
300 g/10½ oz. cooking apples, peeled, cored and chopped
2 onions, peeled and finely chopped
250 g/1½ cups raisins
250 g/1½ cups dates, chopped
700 g/3 cups soft brown sugar
2 garlic cloves, peeled and crushed
1 heaped tablespoon ground ginger
1 tablespoon sea salt

damson chutney

This chutney is rich, dark and heavenly. Damsons are one of my absolute favourite fruits for preserving and lend a superb flavour across the board to any jam, jelly, chutney or pickle that uses them. Removing the stones/pits is a laborious job but is always worth the time. My chosen technique is to cook the fruits first, then remove the stones by hand (usually with the pan on my lap in front of the television). This tedious task has now become part of the chutney-making tradition for me, and since damsons have only a short season once a year, it isn't such a hardship.

1 Place the damsons in a pan with 250 ml/1 cup of the vinegar and cook them until they are soft and bursting. Leave until cool enough to handle, then remove the stones/pits. Place the spices in a piece of muslin/cheesecloth and tie it into a bag with string.

2 Place all the ingredients in a stainless steel preserving pan and bring to the boil, then simmer gently for 2–2½ hours until the chutney Is dark and thick but still juicy, stirring from time to time.

3 Remove the muslin bag, then pour the chutney into hot, sterilized jars (see page 8) and seal (see page 11).

Makes about 1.75 kg/5¼ cups
1 kg/2 lb. 4 oz. green tomatoes
250 g/9 oz. cooking apples, peeled
  and cored
450 g/1 lb. red onions, roughly chopped
200 g/¾ cup soft brown sugar
600 ml/2½ cups malt vinegar

½ teaspoon mustard seeds
½ teaspoon cayenne pepper
1 tablespoon finely grated fresh root ginger
200 g/1¼ cups raisins
3 green chillies/chiles, deseeded and
  finely chopped
1 teaspoon salt

green tomato & red onion chutney

At the end of the growing season, when there is no more heat left outside to ripen the last of the tomatoes, it is time to bring them into the house. If you place them on any empty windowsill you can find, there's a chance that the last precious fruits will slowly turn from green to red. Packing them in boxes, spaced apart in layers with straw or woollen material between them, is another way of ripening them gradually and prolonging the season; but if you have plenty to spare, the still-green ones are just perfect for turning into chutney.

1 To skin the tomatoes place them in a bowl and pour boiling water over them, then leave for a minute or two. The skins should now slide off the fruits when you cut into them with a sharp knife. It is harder to remove the skins when tomatoes are green, so steeping them for longer than usual helps. Chop the tomatoes roughly.

2 Place all the ingredients in a stainless steel preserving pan and bring to the boil. Reduce the heat and simmer until everything is cooked and the chutney has thickened, stirring occasionally.

3 Pour the chutney into hot, sterilized jars (see page 8) and seal (see page 11).

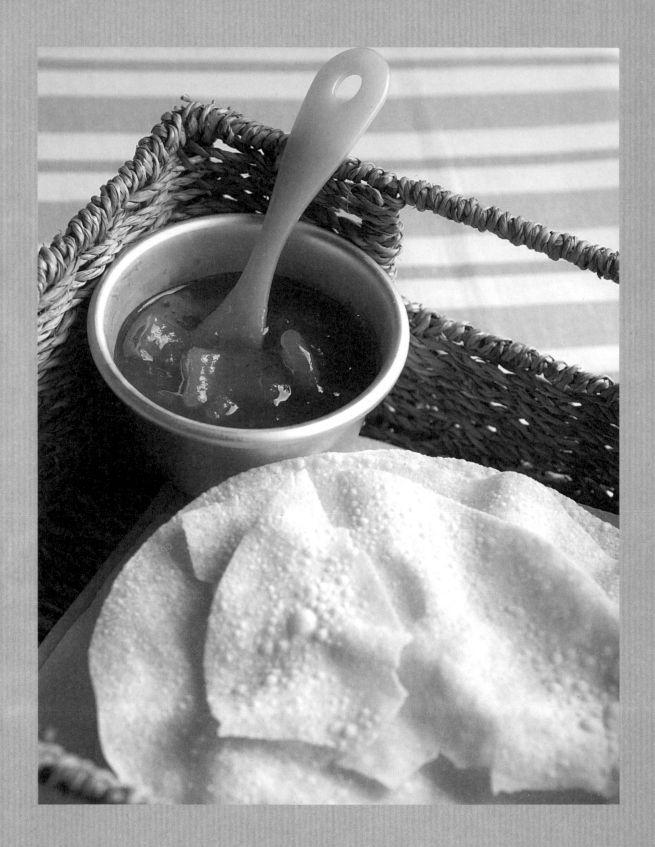

Makes about 1.7 kg/5¼ cups

1.9 kg/4 lb. 3 oz. mangoes (5 or 6 medium
    fruits), skinned and stoned/pitted
2 teaspoons mixed pickling spices
juice and thickly pared rind of 1 orange
350 g/12 oz. onions, finely chopped

300 ml/1¼ cups white wine vinegar
2 garlic cloves
1 tablespoon grated root ginger
2 hot red chillies/chiles, deseeded and
    finely chopped
550 g/2½ cups warmed light muscovado
    sugar (see page 10)

mango chutney

A classic accompaniment to Indian food, you can't beat this sticky sweet chutney. This is a great way of using mangoes when slightly under ripe, if, like me, you aren't ever quite sure whether your mangoes are ripe enough to eat.

1 Cut half of the mango flesh into small pieces and leave the other half in larger chunks. Put the pickling spices and rind pieces in a piece of muslin/cheesecloth and tie it into a bag.

2 Place all the ingredients except the sugar and large mango chunks in a stainless steel preserving pan and simmer gently for 20 minutes until the mango and onions are soft.

3 Add the rest of the mango and simmer gently for another 5 minutes. Add the warmed sugar and stir over a low heat until it has completely dissolved, then boil until the mixture reaches a thick, jam-like consistency, stirring gently and taking care to retain the chunky texture.

4 Remove the muslin bag. Allow the chutney to cool for 10 minutes, then stir again to redistribute the bits.

5 Pour the chutney into hot, sterilized jars (see page 8) and seal (see page 11).

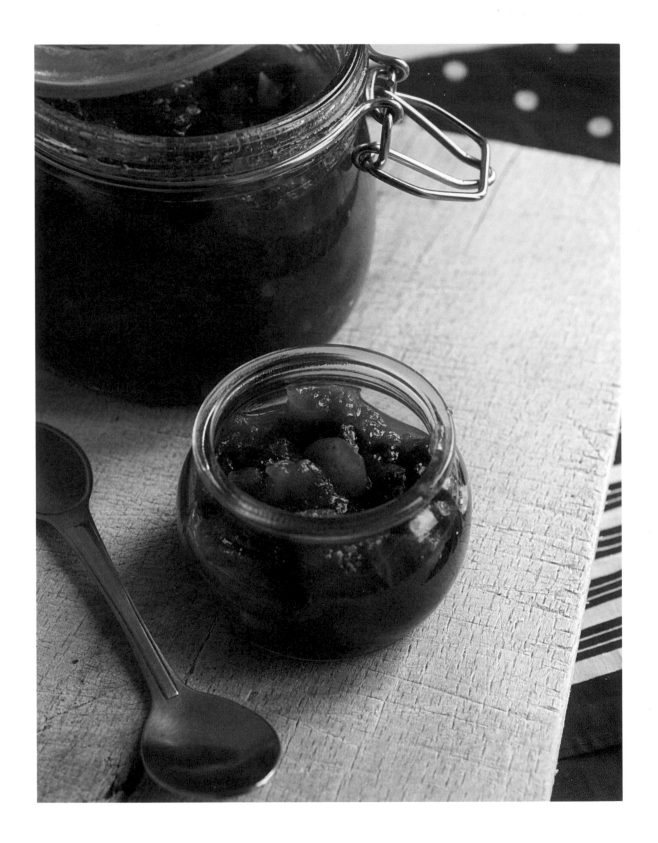

Makes about 1.7 kg/5½ cups

1 kg/2 lb. 4 oz. nectarines, skinned,
  stoned/pitted and roughly chopped
225 g/8 oz. cooking apples, peeled, cored
  and chopped
225 g/8 oz. onions, peeled and finely
  sliced
225 g/1½ cups raisins
350 g/1½ cups light brown sugar
50 g/3 tablespoons stem ginger, finely
  chopped
2 garlic cloves
2 teaspoons sea salt
1 teaspoon cayenne pepper
500 ml/2 cups white wine vinegar

nectarine chutney

Nectarines work so well here. They have just the right amount of sweetness and tartness to make an excellent chutney and this one's a real favourite of mine. I like it with mac and cheese or put in a sandwich with just about anything!

1 Place all the ingredients in a stainless steel preserving pan and stir over a gentle heat to dissolve the sugar. Simmer gently for approximately 1½ hours until the chutney is thick but still juicy, stirring occasionally.

2 Pour the chutney into hot, sterilized jars (see page 8) and seal (see page 11).

peach chutney

Peaches make a straight and worthy substitute here when used instead of nectarines. Use whichever you have in plentiful supply and you won't be disappointed.

Follow the recipe for Nectarine Chutney, substituting peaches for the nectarines. Choose fruits that are firm and only just ripened.

Makes about 1.25 kg/4 cups

1 kg/2 lb. 4 oz. onions, peeled and
finely sliced

2 tablespoons olive oil

500 ml/2 cups red wine vinegar
(or a mixture of red vine vinegar
and balsamic vinegar)

750 g/3 cups muscovado/brown sugar

2 bay leaves

15–20 black peppercorns, crushed

2 teaspoons salt

onion marmalade

Really a chutney or relish, not a marmalade at all. Onion marmalade has become very fashionable in recent years, favoured by chefs and gastro-pubs alike. Generally it isn't a great keeper but this particular version, like other chutneys, will keep well.

1 Separate the onion slices into rings. Heat the oil in a stainless steel preserving pan, add the onion rings and cook them gently for about 20 minutes until they are soft but not browned.

2 Add all the other ingredients and simmer gently for 1–1½ hours until the marmalade is dark and thick but still juicy, stirring occasionally.

3 Pour the marmalade into hot, sterilized jars (see page 8) and seal (see page 11).

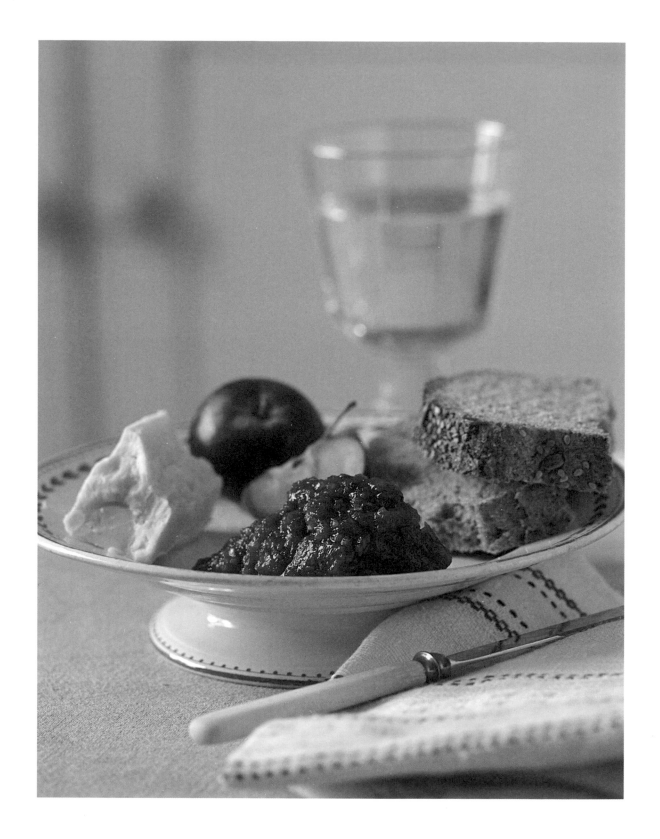

Makes about 2 kg/6¼ cups

1 teaspoon whole allspice
1 teaspoon coriander seeds
2 teaspoons mustard seeds
½ teaspoon cumin seeds
50 g/2 oz. fresh root ginger, bruised
1.5 kg/3 lb. 5 oz. red tomatoes, skinned
   and chopped
500 g/1 lb. 2 oz. cooking apples, peeled,
   cored and diced

500 g/1 lb. 2 oz. onions, peeled and finely
   chopped
2 garlic cloves, peeled and finely chopped
250 ml/1 cup red wine vinegar
1 teaspoon sea salt
200 g/1 cup warmed muscovado/brown
   sugar (see page 10)

red tomato & garlic chutney

This is another easy classic that uses up a glut of tomatoes. In fact, chutney is
so easy to make that it is surprising that anyone ever buys the readymade stuff.
Here, the red fruits and brown sugar give the chutney a lovely rich colour.

1 Place the whole spices and bruised ginger in a piece of
muslin/cheesecloth and tie it into a bag with string.

2 Place all the ingredients except the sugar in a stainless
steel preserving pan and bring to the boil, then simmer until
tender. Add the warmed sugar and stir over a low heat until
all the sugar has dissolved. Turn up the heat and bring to
the boil, then simmer gently for approximately 1½ hours
until the chutney is thick but still juicy, stirring occasionally.

3 Remove the muslin bag, then pour the chutney into hot,
sterilized jars (see page 8) and seal (see page 11).

hot tomato, apple & chilli chutney

As a variation on the previous recipe, this version packs a punch with added oomph supplied by
red hot chillies/chiles and a few extra spices – delicious. Add a dollop to pasta.

Follow Red Tomato and Garlic Chutney, adding 3 or 4 deseeded and finely
chopped hot red chilies/chiles, and include 6 whole cardamom seeds with the
spices and an extra couple of garlic cloves if you wish.

Makes about 1.8 kg/5 cups

900 g/2 lb. apples, peeled and cored

600 ml/2½ cups cider vinegar or malt
  vinegar

55 g/¼ cup pickling spice

1 tablespoon ground ginger

225 g/1½ cups raisins

450 g/2 cups warmed brown sugar
  (see page 10)

2 teaspoons salt

1 red chilli/chile, deseeded and finely
  chopped (optional)

aunt edna's apple chutney

I was given this recipe in the 1970s by a friend's aunt and it was the first chutney I ever made. The results are totally reliable and since then I've made it many times. Thanks, Auntie Edna.

1 Place the apples and vinegar in a stainless steel preserving pan. Tie the pickling spice and ground ginger into a piece of muslin/cheesecloth with string and add to the pan. Cook gently until the apples are tender but still hold their shape.

2 Mince the raisins in a food processor, or chop roughly, and add them to the pan with the sugar, salt and optional chilli/chile; mix well. Bring the chutney to the boil, cooking the mixture until thickened but still juicy, then remove from heat. Remove the spice bundle.

3 Pour the chutney into hot, sterilized jars (see page 8) and seal (see page 11).

Makes about 1.7 kg/5 cups

1 kg/2 lb. 4 oz. cooking apples, peeled,
  cored and chopped

1.2 litres/2½ cups malt vinegar

250 g/9 oz. onions, peeled and chopped

2 teaspoons mustard seeds

1 teaspoon ground ginger

350 g/1½ cups warmed brown sugar (see
  page 10)

350 g/1¾ cups chopped dried dates

1 garlic clove, peeled and chopped

apple & date chutney

Every autumn I end up with bags of apples even though I only possess one small crab apple tree. Friends always have more fruit than they can cope with, so another recipe to use them up is great.

Place the apples, vinegar, onions, mustard seeds and ginger in a stainless steel preserving pan, bring to the boil, then simmer until the apples are soft but still hold their shape. Remove from the heat, add the sugar, dates and garlic, then stir over a gentle heat until the sugar is dissolved. Turn up the heat and bring to the boil, then simmer until the chutney is thick but still juicy. Pot up as above.

Makes about 2 kg/6½ cups

12 peppercorns

2 teaspoons whole allspice

2-cm/¾-inch square piece of fresh root ginger, bruised

750 g/1 lb. 10 oz. pumpkin, peeled, deseeded and cut into chunks

450 g/1 lb. cooking apples, peeled, cored and finely chopped

50 g/2 tablespoons finely chopped stem ginger

350 g/12 oz. shallots, peeled, cored and finely chopped

200 g/1½ cups sultanas/golden raisins, chopped

2 garlic cloves, finely chopped

2 teaspoons salt

600 ml/2½ cups malt or cider vinegar

400 g/scant 2 cups warmed soft brown sugar (see page 10)

pumpkin chutney

With their wonderful shapes, textures and vibrant colours, pumpkins and squashes are always so visually appealing and their flesh gives this chutney a colourful look and sweeter flavour – always a good thing.

1 Place the dry spices and root ginger in a piece of muslin/cheesecloth and tie it into a bag with string. Place all the ingredients except the sugar in a stainless steel preserving pan and bring slowly to the boil, then simmer gently for 20 minutes until the pumpkin and apple are soft.

2 Add the warmed sugar and stir over a gentle heat until all the sugar has dissolved, then turn up the heat and simmer for approximately 1–1½ hours until the chutney is thick but still juicy, stirring occasionally.

3 Remove the muslin bag, then pour the chutney into hot, sterilized jars (see page 8) and seal (see page 11).

marrow chutney

It is great to find 'good ways with marrows', as people who grow squash always seem to end up with a glut of ginormous specimens but without a clue what to do with them. When it comes to preserving, and to chutneys in particular, marrows are a really useful 'filler-outer', in the same way that apples are. However, they are a very watery vegetable, so you need to remove some of this liquid right at the start to concentrate the flavour.

Substitute 750 g/1 lb. 10 oz. marrow for the pumpkin in Pumpkin Chutney. There is no need to add the stem ginger. Place the marrow in a bowl, sprinkle with some salt and leave for 12 hours to draw out the excess water, then rinse thoroughly and drain, then follow the recipe above.

Makes about 1.7 kg/5½ cups
1.3 kg/3 lb. pears, peeled, cored and cut
    into chunks
450 g/1 lb. onions, peeled and chopped
grated rind and juice of 1 lemon
grated rind and juice of 1 orange
225 g/1 scant cup sugar
225 g/1½ cups seedless raisins
300 ml/1¼ cups malt or cider vinegar
1 teaspoon salt
1 teaspoon ground ginger
½ teaspoon cloves

pear chutney

This chutney contains just the right combination of fruitiness and spiciness. I would always recommend that you leave chutney in the larder for a couple of months before eating it and though this pear chutney is no exception, it does taste remarkably good as soon as it is made. Keep it for a while if you can, otherwise devour and enjoy! It is great with cheese.

1 Place all the ingredients in a stainless steel preserving pan and stir over a gentle heat until all the sugar has dissolved. Bring to the boil, then simmer for approximately 2 hours until the chutney is dark and thick but still juicy, stirring occasionally. As with all chutneys, it will thicken up slightly as it cools.

2 Pour the chutney into hot, sterilized jars (see page 8) and seal (see page 11).

pickles

When it comes to pickles, vinegar is the star ingredient. Vinegar comes into its own here and the more matured and spiced it is, the better. You can use any kind of vinegar but cider vinegar goes well with apples and pears, malt vinegar with darker pickles and white wine vinegar helps the colour of ingredients to be seen at their best.

Makes about 800 g/2¼ cups
1 kg/2 lb. 4 oz. crab apples
750 ml/2¾ cups cider or wine vinegar
1 small cinnamon stick

10 cloves
1 teaspoon allspice
800 g/3 cups warmed sugar
 (see page 10)

spiced crab apple pickle

The miniature nature of crab apples makes them very appealing and decorative when used whole, as they are in this pickle. Different varieties of apples will give a very different look to the pickle, and small ruby red apples look particularly cute.

Keep the apples whole and leave the stalks on, then allow a few pickled apples for each serving. The apples require so little preparation that this treatment is well suited to these otherwise fiddly little fruits, but they do need to be in perfect condition before you start. You can use other apple varieties for this pickle if crab apples aren't available. Chop larger fruits, core them and pickle large chunks in the same way. Great served with cheese and crackers.

1 Prick the crab apple skins with a darning needle.

2 Pour the vinegar into a stainless steel pan, add the spices and bring to the boil, then simmer for 5 minutes. Add the apples and simmer until they are tender but still hold their shape. Lift them carefully out of the vinegar using a slotted spoon and pack them into hot, sterilized jars (see page 8).

3 Add the warmed sugar to the vinegar and stir over a low heat until all the sugar has dissolved, then turn up the heat and boil steadily until the vinegar has reduced down by about a third and become syrupy.

4 Pour the hot syrup over the apples so that it completely covers them and seal the jars.

Makes about 1 kg/3 cups
500 ml/2 cups cider vinegar
600 g/2 cups sugar
juice and rind pared from 1 lemon, cut
    into chunks

5 whole allspice berries
2 star anise
2 dried red chillies/chiles
6 black peppercorns
1.5 kg/3 lb. 5 oz. pears

pickled pears

This is such a lovely looking pickle. The pears are wonderful eaten as a relish with cold meats and also work well with cheeses. Use up any of the sweet spiced vinegar remaining in the jar to make salad dressings – try it drizzled over a goat's cheese salad.

1 Place the vinegar, sugar, lemon rind pieces and spices in a stainless steel pan and stir over a gentle heat to dissolve the sugar. Peel and quarter the pears and toss them in the lemon juice to prevent them discolouring.

2 Place the pears in the spiced syrup and simmer gently for approximately 30 minutes until tender and translucent, depending on the ripeness of the fruit. Remove the pear pieces using a slotted spoon and place them in sterilized jars (see page 8).

3 Boil the syrup in the pan to reduce it by half, then pour it and the spices over the pears, making sure they are completely covered with the syrup. Leave until cold, then seal.

Makes about 500 g/1¾ cups
3 plums, halved and stoned/pitted
2 apricots, halved and stoned/pitted
2 figs, halved
2 small pears, peeled and quartered

400 g/1¾ cups sugar
juice of 1 lemon
150 ml/⅔ cup dry white wine
420 g/1 cup honey
50 g/½ cup English mustard powder

mostarda di frutta

If you are unfamiliar with mustard fruits, now is a good time to be introduced. It is a delicious mustard-based condiment with Italian origins. (The name actually comes not from 'mustard' but from 'mosto', which is the unfermented grape juice, reduced to a thick syrup, in which the fruits were originally preserved.) Originally made with quinces or grapes, it can be made using any mixture of fruits, usually pears, plums, peaches, whole cherries and figs.

This pickle can be served chopped over fish and goes well with pork and sausages and strong salty cheeses. Finely chopped mostarda can also be mashed with pumpkin when making a filling for ravioli. Use any leftover syrup in salad dressings and drizzle over bitter salad leaves.

1 Preheat the oven to 100°C fan/120°C/250°F/Gas ½.

2 Place all the fruit in a stainless steel pan and add just enough water to cover. Add the sugar and lemon juice and stir gently to dissolve the sugar, then turn up the heat and boil to make a thin syrup. Simmer over a low heat for about 10 minutes, so the fruit pieces are cooked but stay intact.

3 Remove the fruit pieces with a slotted spoon, draining them well, and place on a baking sheet. Cook in the oven for about 45–50 minutes until the fruits are dry.

4 Add the wine and honey to the syrup and simmer over a low heat for 10–15 minutes to reduce it down. Add the mustard powder and mix well.

5 Put the fruit pieces into hot, sterilized jars (see page 8) and pour over the syrup to cover. Leave until cold, then seal.

Makes about 500 g/1¾ cups
450 g/1 lb. damsons
225 g/1 cup sugar
2 short cinnamon sticks

6 cloves
4 pieces of root ginger, about
  2 cm/¾ inch square
malt vinegar (for quantity see step 1)

pickled damsons

This traditional method for pickling damsons is well worth the effort. You could cut down the amount of straining and boiling, and you would still get a delicious pickle – if not quite as rich.

1 Preheat the oven to 130°C fan/150°C/300°F/Gas 2. Put the damsons into a ceramic dish and sprinkle with sugar. Tie the spices in a piece of muslin/cheesecloth. Pour enough vinegar onto the fruit to cover, add the spices, then put the dish at the bottom of the oven for 20 minutes until the fruits feel soft and the juices start to run.

2 Allow to cool, then strain the juice into a pan and add the spices. Bring to the boil, then discard the spices and pour the liquid over the damsons. Repeat this straining and boiling process (without spices) each day for 10 days, then leave the damsons immersed in the juice for another 7 days, refrigerating between processing.

3 Strain the damsons again and pack into a hot, sterilized jar (see page 8). Bring the rich, syrupy juice to the boil and pour over the damsons. Leave until cold, then seal the jar.

Makes about 500 g/1¾ cups
450 g/1 lb. apricots
225 g/1 cup sugar
2 short cinnamon sticks
2 cloves

2 pieces of root ginger, about
  2 cm/¾ inch square
½ teaspoon whole allspice
wine vinegar (for quantity see
  step 1 above)

pickled apricots

This is another versatile alternative, where the sweetness of the fruit is perfectly offset by the sharpness of the vinegar. Out of season, make using dried apricots instead.

Follow step 1 above, using the apricots and different spice quantities. Remove the apricots with a slotted spoon and pack into a sterilized jar (see page 8). Boil the remaining liquid until it becomes syrupy; discard the spice bag, then pour the liquid over the apricots. Leave in the fridge overnight. Next day, remove the apricots from the jar and strain the syrup into a pan. Put the apricots back in the jar and bring the syrup to the boil, then pour over the apricots. Leave until cold, then seal.

Makes about 750 g/3 pints
8 or 9 small lemons
sea salt (for quantity see step 2)
1 bay leaf

1 small cinnamon stick
a few coriander seeds
1 dried chilli/chile

preserved lemons

Preserved lemons are an essential ingredient in Moroccan and North African cuisine. They can be added to casseroles and salads and have a fragrant, sweet and sour taste. Once pickled you eat the whole fruit, rind and all. As the lemons are used, simply add more salt and lemon juice to the jar so the fruits stay immersed.

1 Cut off the stalk end of each lemon; then, holding it upright, slice it down in quarters to within 2 cm/¾ inch of the base so it opens out but doesn't come apart.

2 Pack the sea salt in between the cuts, using approximately 1 tablespoonful for each lemon, then pack the lemons as tightly as you can into a large (approximately 1 litre/1¾ pints) sterilized wide-necked jar, pushing them down to encourage them to release their juice. Distribute the other flavourings (left whole) among the lemons. Close the jar and leave it overnight.

3 The next day, press the lemons down more so they release more juice. Continue doing this each day for the next 3 days until the lemons are completely submerged in the juice, topping up if necessary with more lemon juice.

4 Seal the jar and leave the lemons for 1 month, by which time they should be soft and ready to use.

5 Store the lemons in the refrigerator, where they will keep for at least 6 months. Rinse off excess salt before using.

Makes about 2.25 kg/7 cups

500 g/1 lb. 2 oz. cauliflower, broken into florets

225 g/8 oz. runner/green beans, topped and tailed, then sliced

225 g/8 oz. green tomatoes, cut into chunks

500 g/1 lb. 2 oz. shallots, peeled and halved if small

1 kg/2 lb. 4 oz. marrow flesh, diced

400 g/⅞ cup salt

1.7 litres/6¾ cups malt vinegar

200 g/⅞ cup sugar

20 g/1 heaped tablespoon English mustard powder

2 teaspoons mustard seeds

1 teaspoon ground ginger

4 small dried chillies/chiles, crushed

40 g/¼ cup cornflour/cornstarch

2 tablespoons ground turmeric

piccalilli

Piccalilli is a good way of preserving homegrown seasonal vegetables, and the medley can be changed to suit what you have available at the time. It is another resourceful way of using up marrow, or you can substitute courgettes/zucchini – both crops that often fit into the 'feast or famine' category: when available, there is usually an overabundance.

1 Mix all the vegetables together and layer them in a bowl, sprinkling salt in between the layers, then leave overnight. The next day, drain the vegetables, rinse thoroughly to remove all the salt and drain again.

2 Pour the vinegar into a pan and stir in the sugar, mustard powder and seeds, ginger and dried chillies/chiles. Add the vegetables and simmer until just tender but still in chunks. You can choose the texture of pickle you like best by keeping the vegetables crunchy or soft.

3 Blend the cornflour/cornstarch and turmeric with a few tablespoons of vinegar from the pan and stir this into the mixture, then boil for 2–3 minutes.

4 Pour the piccalilli into hot, sterilized jars (see page 8) and leave until cold, then seal.

Makes about 1 kg/3 cups
1 kg/2 lb. 4 oz. pickling shallots
250 g/½ cup salt

600 ml/2½ cups pickling vinegar
(see page 13)

pickled shallots

Pickled onions are a classic pickle and one that seems to be popular with children and adults alike. They go with just about anything, but a simple ploughman's lunch made up of a piece of crusty bread, a wedge of strong cheese and some pickled onions is a combination that is hard to beat. To be sure that your onions retain that initial crunch, they need to be marinated in brine for a few days before being packed into jars and covered in spiced vinegar. Apart from that, this pickle has to be the easiest there is and you should always keep a few jars on the pantry shelf.

1 Place the shallots in a large bowl without skinning them. Make the brine by dissolving half of the salt in 1 litre/quart water, then pour this over the shallots and leave for 12 hours. Drain and skin the shallots.

2 Make up a second batch of brine using the remaining salt and the same amount of water, pour it over the shallots and leave for a further 2–3 days.

3 Meanwhile, if you don't already have some pickling vinegar steeping in a cupboard, make a batch of the quick version a while before the brining period is due to finish and leave until cold.

4 Drain and rinse the salt from the onions and pack them tightly into jars. Pour the cold pickling vinegar over them so that they are completely covered. Cover and seal the jars. The shallots will keep their flavour and crispness for up to 6 months after bottling.

sweet & sour onions

This pickle benefits from using a sweeter vinegar than the previous recipe, to give a delectable sweet and sour tang. It is very easy to make.

Here the onions are pickled in a sweet pickling vinegar. Follow the recipe above, but use either some sweet pickling vinegar already steeping in a cupboard or make up a batch of the quicker alternative instead (see page 13 for both recipes).

useful addresses

Many local hardware stores and well-stocked cook shops sell all the bits and pieces you need for jam making, from preserving pans to jam jars and labels. Here are a few online companies that also stock the things you will need.

www.lakeland.co.uk
www.waresofknutsford.co.uk
www.allamericancanner.com
www.canningpantry.com
www.freshpreserving.com

author's acknowledgements

For my mum, Alice Nicol, for her unconditional love, help and support, without which I would be lost.

Thanks to Sue Rowlands for bringing order to the proceedings, not to mention lovely props, a fabulous eye for detail and general encouragement and friendship.
   Thanks also to Cindy Richards for giving me the opportunity to write a book on a subject I love, as well the rest of the Ryland Peters & Small team: Sally Powell and Gillian Haslam for patiently pulling it all together, Alison Bolus and Eleanor Van Zandt for making sense of it all, and Jane Smith for her lovely drawings.
   Thanks to Deborah Schneebeli-Morrell for making whitecurrant and chilli jam using her own homegrown fruit, and to friends and neighbours for their help and support, especially Judy Dann for our foodie conversations and for sending me surprise recipes in the post on many occasions.
   Finally, a massive thank you to Chris and Lisa for helping me keep life on an even keel so I could get on with the book, and to my friend, Lindsey Stock, without whose help the book would not have been possible.

index